CIBL

Cue Intuition Before Leaving Earth

Introduction

Cible: Cue Intuition Before Leaving Earth & also meaning target. Cible is a collection of my poetry, I have written throughout my lifetime. Throughout every emotion, situation, or knowledge I've learned. I put in a poem to express myself. I have always been a fan of rap / hip hop. I truly feel I grew up with hip hop from the begin of its reign. At one point I did want to become a rapper but I was too shy. I gained a love for poetry in school. I would of never thought or dream to write a poetry book. The thought came to me a couple years ago. I was scrolling through my writings. I knew I no longer wanted to be a rapper, but I still wanted to share my work to the world. My collection go back as far as my high school days. I still have a couple of my class assignment poems I wrote. I seriously started writing outside of being in school in 1996. I had a collection of work from 1996 to 1999 lost. That is still one of the most painful experience, I experience to this day. I almost gave up writing but I continued. It took me longer to build up my body of work again. Now I have a large body of work & I will be putting my poetry out in a series of books. I feel it's my destiny to put this body of work out. I hope I can enlighten, inspire, & entertain all my readers. I was always told the truth hurts but then it will set you free. Everything isn't for everybody. Through life experience, I found out it's impossible to please everyone.

While making one group of people happy, you could be upsetting another group at the same time. I figured life is like a Rubik Cube. I follow my intuition & always remain righteous. I pray that you enjoy my work.

ISBN: 9798856376592

DEDICATION

I dedicate this to my Mom Perri Channelle, my sister Lashonya Owens, my kids
Edwin Brooks Jr aka Lil E
aka Mookie, Jaleb Brooks, Janaya Mackey, Kamaria Bailey, Ja'kira Cue, my kids'
mothers, Katina Mickens,
Shonda Filer rest in peace, My brother Rhyeaul Cairwell aka Bobe, TALONDA,
my niece Tori, My nephews
Tre, Thomas, Tahj, all my family cousins, aunt, uncles. And everybody that
supported me through this
process. It's been a long journey. This is my life and experiences. This is the first
book of many, If The All
Most High grant with time to complete the others.

CONTENTS

Phase I

THE LIGHT

Phase II

The Awakening

Phase III

The Transition

Phase IV

Philosophical

Phase IX

LIFE

ACKNOWLEDGMENTS

First and foremost The All Most High, for blessing me with the knowledge, wisdom, and dedication to accomplish completing Cible. This has been years in the making, sparking from an idea after seeing all my writings. I no longer wanted to be a performer but I knew my writings was inspirational, enlighten, and still needed to be shared. My family, friends, supporters, Allpoetry.com, Poetizer, Facebook Poetry Communities, & Amazon and Kindle for giving me the platform to present my writings from my soul.

PHASE I. THE LIGHT

New Beginnings...

New Beginnings, New Beginnings, in my old life I was winning.

Things happen for a reason, so I had a bad ending.

They say what don't kill you, only make you strong.

& I been through so much drama, I got strength like King Kong.

I never gave up, no matter the pressure I carried on.

They say, GOD will never put too much on you that you couldn't bear, so I'm here where I belong.

So, I stay humble, & remain to be positive.

And be the best man I can be, for the rest of this life I live.

Now I got to love from a distance, & learn tough love.

I'll still have excellent service, for any of you cove.

Now I'm focused on me, being the best, I can be.

I sacrificed the best years of my life, but I have more in me.

I had no control in the beginning, but I can write the end.

& mine is going to end happy, without no sin.

I'll be there for the ones that's there for me.

For wisdom is better than jewels, & all that you may desire can't compare to me

Know Thyself

I'm enlighten & blessed & know that I Am great.

The people you are better than, you receive nothing but hate.

Even with people having more than you.

The one thing they can't buy, is being you.

My heart is pure, I love life & wish well on everybody I know.

Most of the time I didn't receive the same in return, but that's the way life go.

I Am who I Am Jr, I Am the Son of GOD.

Never going with the hype, I'm against all odds.

I love me, I'll never trade my life for nothing in this world.

All I need is me, not no homeboys or a main girl.

I thank The Most High for my family, that really care for me.

& For them & The Most High, I'm gone be all I can Be.

I careless what they think or say, because I know thyself.

I'd feel like I succeeded, passing on knowledge & wealth.

From A King to A GOD

From being caught up in the flesh,
trying to please man & sit on a
throne.
To finding out my axioms is of The
All, my destiny is out of this o-zone.
My quest was to make this world
better or spark the mind that will do
it.
My glory come from a higher power,
not man contemporary history, & the
small percentage of people
That knew it.
I have Imparted the knowledge of
constellations Sirius A & B, like I
from the Dogon tribe.
With the spirit of the Most High,
love, knowledge, & health is my vibe.
& to be in tune with nature of the
earth.

So, this world would still be around
for my great, great, great, grandkids
birth.
I'm not conforming to this world; I'm
thinking far & beyond.
I Am now the chess board, from
being a king from a pawn.
This is God's plan it's in my DNA,
for me to become a Sun.
& Become my own galaxy creating
life & enlighten everyone.
I keep my chakras aligned & my
vibrations high.
Anything's possible gain knowledge,
focus & try.
Stay in tune with God & your soul
will never die.
When this is all over, to your next
destination, you will fly.

PSALMS 725.

TO YOU I LIFT UP MY EYES, O YOU WHO ARE
ENTHRONED IN THE HEAVENS.
I GOT TO DELIVER THIS WORD, AS IF I WAS A
REVEREND.
TO YOU, O GOD I LIFT UP MY SOUL.
REMEMBER YOUR MERCY, O LORD AND YOUR
STEADFAST LOVE, FOR ME HAVE BEEN FROM
OF OLD.
MAY THE MOST HIGH ANSWER ME IN THE DAY
OF TROUBLE.
NO WEAPON FORMED AGAINST ME SHALL
PROSPER, FEEL LIKE I'M IN A BUBBLE.
LET THEM BE PUT TO SHAME AND DISHONOR
WHO SEEK AFTER MY LIFE.
LET THEM BE TURNED BACK AND
DISAPPOINTED THAT COME AT ME TRIFE.
CONTEND O'LORD WITH THOSE WHO
CONTEND WITH ME.
FIGHT AGAINST THOSE WHO FIGHT AGAINST
ME.
LET DESTRUCTION COME UPON HIM WHEN HE
DOES NOT KNOW IT.
AND LET THE NET THAT HE HID ENSNARE HIM
FOR IT.
THEY REPAY ME EVIL FOR GOOD MY SOUL IS
BEREFT.
MY LIFE WAS ON DISPLAY BUT NOW IT'S GONE
BY THEFT.
LET THEM BE TURNED BACK AND BROUGHT TO
DISHONOR, WHO DELIGHT IN MY HURT, AND
MY PAIN.

I SAY TO THE BOASTFUL, DO NOT BOAST AND
THE WICKED; DO NOT LIFT YOUR HORN, IF YOU
ARE SANE.
LIKE PROFANE MOCKERS AT A FEAST, THEY
GNASH AT ME WITH THEIR TEETH.
THEN THEY OPENED WITH THEIR MOUTHS
AGAINST ME, THEY SAY AHA AHA, I'M IN
DISBELIEF.
AT MY STUMBLING THEY REJOICED AND
GATHERED TOGETHER AGAINST ME.
WRETCHES WHOM I DIDN'T KNOW TORE
WITHOUT CEASING OR KNOWING ME.
O'LORD HAVE MERCY UPON ME, FOR I HAVE
HAD MORE THAN ENOUGH OF CONTEMPT.
MY SOUL HAS HAD MORE THAN ENOUGH
SCORN TO THOSE WHO ARE PROUD AT EASE OF
THE CONTEMPT.
THEY ONLY MADE ME STRONGER, WHEN THEY
THOUGHT THEY SEALED MY FATE.
PRAISE TO THE ALL MOST HIGH, YES GOD IS
GREAT.

AIN'T NO RIGHT WAY TO DO WRONG.

AIN'T NO RIGHT WAY TO DO WRONG, SO DO
RIGHT THE FIRST TIME.
PLAN, PLOT & STRATEGIZE, SO YOU CAN
INCLINE.
EASY COME EASY GO, WHY LIVE FOR
TEMPORARY SUCCESS.
WHY GO NOWHERE FAST, THEN AT THE END
SETTLE FOR LESS.
DOING RIGHT TO SOME PEOPLE SEEM LIKE A
SIN.
BUT CRY & COMPLAIN WHEN THE WRONG
CONSEQUENCES KICK IN.
WHEN THEY BE ON TOP LIFE IS ALL GOOD,
NOTHING'S WRONG THAT THEY CAN DO.
WHEN THEY LOSE IT ALL LIFE'S A B!+<H, &
EVERYONE AGAINST YOU.
TO MANY MAJOR SETBACKS, TO BECOME MINOR
& CAN'T COME BACK.
KEEP DOING THE SAME THING, GETTING THE
SAME RESULTS & THAT'S A FACT.
NOTHING IN THIS WORLD YOU CAN'T DO, TAKE
YOUR TIME DO IT RIGHT.
ANYTHING WORTH ACHIEVING IS GOING TO
TAKE A LONG & HARD FIGHT.
LIVE LIFE WRONG YOU WILL GET THE WRONG
RESULTS.
TIME IS MONEY, MONEY IS TIME TO WASTE
MINE IS AN INSULT.
WHY WASTE YOUR TIME DOING WRONG, TO
HAVE NOTHING AT THE END.
LEAVE A LEGACY FOR YOUR KIDS TO CARRY
ON, OR EITHER TO BEGIN.

BIG SIS

I DEEPLY APPRECIATE EVERYTHING YOU
DONE, BEING HERE EVERY STEP OF THE WAY.
I PRAY IN THIS LIFETIME, BACK TO YOU
EVERYTHING I CAN REPAY.
I FEEL LIKE MALCOLM X AND YOU ARE HIS BIG
SISTER ELLA.
WITHOUT YOU IN MY LIFE, WHERE I WOULD BE
I COULD NOT TELL YA.
WHEN I GET OUT, I'LL BE RIGHT BACK ON TASK.
ANYTHING FROM ME, YOU CAN GET IT IF YOU
ASK.
CONGRATULATIONS ON YOUR GRANDSON, I
CAN'T WAIT TO MEET HIM.
SPOILED IS THE WAY, I KNOW YOU GONE TO
TREAT HIM.
I PRAY EVERY DAY, THAT THIS BE OVER SOON.
I PRAY TO REDEEM MYSELF & MY LIFE WILL
RESUME.
I THANK YOU FOR THE WORDS OF
ENCOURAGEMENT, TO HELP MAINTAIN.
WITHOUT YOU BEING HERE FOR ME, I'D
PROBABLY WENT INSANE.
THROUGHOUT THIS DIRE SITUATION, I TURNED
TO A BETTER MAN.
I WANT LET NOTHING IN LIFE AGAIN, DETOUR
ME FROM GOD PLAN.
I TRULY THANK YOU FOR EVERYTHING, & YOU
ARE TRULY MISS.
YOU ARE IN PRAYS EVERY DAY, I LOVE YOU BIG
SIS.

DEAR MOMMA TOO,

DEAR MOM I LOVE & THANK YOU FROM THE
BOTTOM OF MY HEART.
EVEN THOUGH WE HIT SOME ROCKY ROADS,
IT'S NEVER LATE TO RESTART.
& GET BACK ON THE RIGHT PATH.
& LOOK BACK ON THEM TIMES, & HAVE A
GOOD LAUGH.
I KNOW I GOT TO STAY IN YOUR PRAYERS
EVERY DAY.
BECAUSE AT TIMES I THINK I CANNOT MAKE IT,
THE MOST HIGH FIND A WAY.
PLEASE FORGIVE ME FOR ALL THE
HEARTACHES, I MIGHT OF CAUSE.
I WAS YOUNG AND AMBITIOUS, BUT STILL A
LOST CAUSE.
I WAS HOLDING ON TO TOO MUCH ANGER.
ONLY TO MYSELF, I WAS A DANGER.
INSTEAD OF LOOKING IN THE MIRROR, I WAS
POINTING FINGERS.
THE FURTHER I MOVED AWAY, LIFE GOT
STRANGER.
NOW I'M BACK TO GIVE YOU ALL MY LOVE.
AND GIVE YOU THE BEST LIFE, UNTIL WE HIT
THE HEAVENS UP ABOVE.
DON'T WORRY ABOUT A THING.
I GOT YOU, MY QUEEN.
FOR THE REST OF MY DAYS, I'LL BE THE BEST
HUMAN BEING.
I TRULY THANK YOU FOR EVERYTHING YOU
DONE, & THE LIFE YOU GAVE ME.
SINCERELY YOUR SON, MOM MS. PERRI LEE..

VEGAN LIFE...

BECOMING VEGAN IS THE BEST DECISION I
EVER MADE.
YOUR FOOD IS YOUR MEDICINE, DO NOT GET
PLAYED,
INTO EATING UNHEALTHY FOODS THAT TASTE
GOOD, BUT DO YOUR BODY NO GOOD.
DON'T WAIT UNTIL YOU CATCH CANCER,
DIABETES, OR HIGH BLOOD PRESSURE AND
THEN WISH YOU WOULD,
OF ATE HEALTHIER, AFTER LEARNING WHAT
YOU EAT IS THE CAUSE OF MOST DISEASE.
GETTING SECOND HAND PROTEIN FROM MEAT
IS JUST A TEASE.
PLUS, WE HAVE LONG INTESTINES NOT SHORT
THAT'S NOT DESIGNED TO EAT MEAT.
PLUS, WE DON'T HAVE LONG K-9'S BUT
HERBIVORE TEETH.
EATING FLESH BUT DON'T LIKE DRINKING
BLOOD, IS LIKE EATING ORANGES BUT NOT
LIKEN ORANGE JUICE.
EAT FRUITS, VEGETABLES, & NUTS TO GIVE
YOUR LIFE A BOOST.
TO MAKE MEAT EATABLE, YOU MUST SEASON IT
WITH HERB AND SPICES.
EAT TO LIVE NOT LIVE TO EAT, TO MAKE YOUR
MIND AND BODY THE NICEST.
YOU ARE WHAT YOU EAT, YOUR HEALTH IS
YOUR WEALTH.
WHY KEEP POISONING YOUR BODY UNTIL
YOUR DEATH.
I AM 7 YEARS AND GOING UNTIL THE END OF
MY FATE.

EVERY DAY THE MOST HIGH BLESS ME WITH
LIFE, I'M FEELING GOOD FEELING GREAT.

CO.RONA VI.RUS D.ISEASE - 2019

DID IT COME FROM CHINA LIVE STOCK
MARKET, A LABORATORY, OR SOME BATS.
BROUGHT TO THE UNITED STATES BY A NEW
YORK LAWYER EFFECTING EVERYBODY
ACCEPT THE RATS.
THEN SOMEHOW IT GOT INTO ALL THE OLD
FOLK HOMES.
THE WORLD WAS IN CHAOS NOBODY KNOWS
WHAT'S GOING ON.
SENIOR CITIZENS IN HOMES RARELY MOBILE
BUT THEY STARTED A TRAVEL BAN.
AT FIRST, THEY DIDN'T MANDATE MASK BUT
THEY TOLD US WASH OUR HANDS.
AFTER SPRING BREAK AND MARDI GRAS
CORONA WAS OUT OF CONTROL.
HOT SPOTS EVERYWHERE, SCHOOL CANCELED,
THE GOVERNMENT TAKES CONTROL.
IT STARTED WITH CURFEWS, AND THEN THEY
HAD ROAD BLOCKS.
FORTUNE 500 C.E.O'S RESIGNING, POLITICIANS
SELLING THEIR STOCKS.
THEN THEY SHUT DOWN CITIES UNLESS YOU
WERE AN ESSENTIAL WORKER ON A JOB.
EVERY DAY THEY GIVE YOU THE STATISTICS OF

VICTIMS OF COVID-19 WHO LIFE BEEN ROB.
EVERY NEWS REPORT SAYS THAT DAY HAD THE
MOST DEATHS, & IT HAVEN'T HIT ITS PEAK.
NOW MASK IS MANDATORY, NO ALCOHOL,
SANITIZERS, TISSUE, & PAPER TOWELS ON
STORE SHELVES FOR WEEKS.
EVERYTHING CLOSED ALL YOU HAVE IS
AMAZON & WAL-MART.
IT'S BETTER TO BE SAFE THAN SORRY IF YOU
SMART.
THEN THEY STARTED OPENING THE CITY IN
SEVERAL PHASES.
NOT KNOWING IF LIFE WILL EVER BE NORMAL
AGAIN, OR THESE ARE THE NEW DAYS.
THEN THEY SPENT MONTHS TALKING ABOUT
VACCINES.
AND ISSUING STIMULUS CHECKS TO TRY TO
BETTER EVERYTHING.
PROFESSIONAL & COLLEGE TEAMS PLAYING IN
EMPTY ARENAS AND STADIUMS.
QUARANTINING FOR MONTHS AT HOME WITH
NOTHING TO DO, BUT LOOK AT NEWS FEELING
DUMB.
THEY FINALLY APPROVED THE VACCINES, BUT
YOU NEED TWO SHOTS.
SIDE EFFECTS PEOPLE ARE DYING OR HAVING
BLOOD CLOTS.
IT SEEMS SO UNREAL IT'S LIKE A BAD DREAM.
I MISS THE WORLD BEFORE COVID-19...

TRULY TRULY I SAY TO YOU…

TRULY TRULY I SAY TO YOU, I AM WHO I AM, DO
YOU KNOW WHO YOU BE.
A GOOD HEART & HIGH SPIRIT IS THE MAKING
OF ME.
TRULY TRULY I SAY TO YOU, I'M HATED FOR
BEING SO GREAT.
INSTEAD OF THEM TRYING TO LEARN FROM
ME, THEY WANT TO SEAL MY FATE.
I'M GOD SON, PURE AT HEART WITH NO BAD
INTENTIONS.
BEFORE LEAVING EARTH, YOU SHOULD LEARN
THE BASIC INTUITIONS.
TRULY TRULY I SAY TO YOU, WHEN YOU
RIDICULE AND TRY TO PULL ME DOWN, YOU
JUST MAKE ME GREATER.
HOW DO YOU SAY YOU LOVE GOD, WHEN YOU
ARE ENVIOUS & NOTHING BUT A HATER.
EVERY TIME THEY SWEAR, I'M DOWN & OUT, &
THINK THAT I'M THROUGH.
THIS IS GOD GIFT ALL I GOT TO DO IS SHOW UP,
TRULY TRULY IS WHAT I SAID TO YOU.
DO NOT REPAY EVIL WITH EVIL, JUST KILL
THEM WITH SUCCESS.
AIM FOR THE STARS, NEVER SETTLE FOR LESS.
TAKE TIME TO MEDITATE, SO YOU RELIEVE
YOUR STRESS.
TRULY TRULY I SAY TO YOU, YOU ARE SEEKING
ME BECAUSE YOU SAW SIGNS.
REAL RECOGNIZE REAL LIKEWISE, & A LOT
YOU OF ARE IGNORANT OR BLIND.
TRULY TRULY I SAY TO YOU, WHOEVER

BELIEVES HAS ETERNAL LIFE.
YOUR FATHERS ATE THE MANNA IN THE
WILDERNESS & THEY DIED, I AM THE BREAD OF
LIFE.

LETTER TO MY SON EDWIN BROOKS JR.
3-16.

MARCH SIXTEEN THE DAY I HAD MY FIRST-
BORN SON, & BECAME A MAN.
HE WAS BORN THREE MONTHS EARLY; THIS IS
GOD'S PLAN.
HE IS MY JUNIOR, MY LIL MINI ME.
I HAD TO GET FOCUS & BECOME ALL THAT I
CAN BE.
SEVENTEEN FRESH OUT OF HIGH SCHOOL,
NOW I'M A DAD.
PLUS, I WAS FRESH OUT THE STREETS, GOOD
KID FORCE TO LIVE BAD.
WORDS COULD NOT EXPLAIN THE JOY, I GOT
FOR MY BOY.
SEEM LIKE YESTERDAY I WAS BUYING HIM JAYS
& HIS FAVORITE TOY.
I MISS MY HIGH SCHOOL GRADUATION,
BECAUSE I HAD TO BABY SIT HIM.
HE REPAID ME 18 YEARS LATER, BY
GRADUATING I GOT TO WATCH HIM.
A GREAT KID HE NEVER GOT IN TROUBLE, OR
CAUSE ME ANY PROBLEMS AT ALL.
IF HE EVER NEEDS ME, I'LL ALWAYS BE THERE
IF HE EVER CALLS.

NOW MY BOY'S A MAN, IT'S SO HARD TO SAY
GOODBYE TO YESTERDAY.
I MISS TAKING HIM TO THE PARK, SO
BASKETBALL WE CAN PLAY.
BECOMING HIS DAD IS THE GREATEST GIFT
GOD EVER GAVE ME.
1997 THE 16TH DAY IN THE MONTH NUMBER
THREE..

LETTER TO MY SON JALEB BROOKS
8-24

THE BIRTH OF JALEB BROOKS EIGHT TWENTY-
FOUR ZERO ONE.
THE COMING OF MY SECOND BORN SON.
HE LIT UP MY WORLD LIKE THE SUN.
I WISH I COULD REWIND THE DAYS WHEN WE
HAD SO MUCH FUN.
A DIRECT REFLECTION OF ME, I WAS TOLD
LOOK LIKE I SPIT HIM OUT.
I CANNOT DENY HIM, HE IS MINE WITHOUT A
DOUBT.
MY BABY BOY, A PROUD FATHER FILLED WITH
SO MUCH JOY.
I WISH I COULD TURN BACK THE HANDS OF
TIME WHEN YOU WANTED GAMES AND TOY.
YOU NEVER CAUSED ME PROBLEMS, OR GOT IN
ANY TROUBLE.
IF YOU EVER NEED ME, I WOULD BE THERE IN
A DOUBLE.

AN INCREDIBLY WISE & INTELLIGENT YOUNG
MAN, ALWAYS DID GOOD IN SCHOOL.
ALWAYS DID WHAT WAS RIGHT, NEVER CARED
FOR BEING COOL.
I AM IMMENSELY PROUD OF YOU SON, & I LOVE
YOU TO DEATH.
I WILL ALWAYS BE HERE IF YOU CALL, UNTIL
MY VERY LAST BREATH.
IT HAS BEEN A LONG TIME, SINCE WE HAD
THAT FATHER & SON BOND.
I HOPE WE CAN REKINDLE OUR RELATIONSHIP
AND BE CLOSE FROM HERE AND BEYOND.

LETTER TO MY DAUGHTER JANAYA
8-13

MY FIRST-BORN DAUGHTER, DADDIES' PRIDE &
JOY PRINCESS.
ANYTHING IN THIS WORLD FOR YOU, I JUST
WANT THE BEST.
TWO YEARS UNKNOWN, BUT THIS IS GOD PLAN.
I HAD TO GET MYSELF TOGETHER & BE THE
MAN.
BECAUSE MY PRINCESS WILL NEVER HAVE TO
WANT FOR NOTHING.
YOU ARE BEAUTIFUL & INTELLIGENT A TRUE
BLESSING.
ME & YOUR MOM SUPER RARELY GOT ALONG, &
IT WAS NOT ON THE FAULT OF ME.
BUT I NEVER LET THAT MISGUIDE ME FROM
BEING THE BEST DAD I CAN BE.

FOR YOU I WOULD GIVE MY LIFE OR DO LIFE IN
JAIL.
IF ANYONE TRY TO HARM YOU, I WILL NEED
BAIL.
WE HAD SOME GREAT FATHER & DAUGHTER
MOMENTS; I WOULDN'T TRADE FOR NOTHING
IN THE WORLD.
JANAYA MACKEY MY FIRST LITTLE GIRL.
THAT MADE ME FEEL LIKE A PROUD DAD, MY
LITTLE ANGEL GIFT FROM GOD.
I WILL NEVER LET YOU DOWN OR FAIL YOU, I'M
GOING TO COMPLETE MY JOB.
TO BE THE BEST FATHER THE MOST HIGH,
BLESS ME TO BE.
AFTER SEEING THAT YOU ARE STRAIGHT, I CAN
REST IN PEACE FOR ETERNITY

LETTER TO MY DAUGHTER KAMARIA BAILEY
3-23

I REMEMBER THE DAY I FIRST HELD YOU &
LOOKED YOU IN YOUR EYES.
A PERFECT LIKENESS TO ME, MY BABY GIRL I
CAN'T DENY.
I ONLY WANTED THE BEST FOR YOU, SINCE
YOUR BIRTH.
NOTHING IN THIS WORLD TO ME, IS MORE
THAN YOUR WORTH.
THE BEST DAD I EVER TRIED TO BE; I WAS
THERE ANY TIME YOU ALL CALL.

INCLUDING MY LIFE, ANYTHING YOU WANT
FROM ME, I'LL GIVE YOU MY ALL.
THIS IS ALL ABOUT YOU, YOU ARE MY PRINCESS.
ANYTHING YOU PUT YOUR MIND TO, I KNOW
YOU WOULD BE THE BEST.
ANYTIME I WAS WITH YOU, IT WAS A PRICELESS
MOMENT.
2021 YOUR FIRST BIRTHDAY I WASN'T THERE, SO
IN THIS POEM I'LL HAVE TO VENT.
WE GOING THRU SOME TERRIBLE TIMES, I
KNOW ONE DAY THINGS WILL BE BETTER.
IT ISN'T NO HATE IN MY HEART, THAT I'M
POURING OUT IN THIS LETTER.
FROM MY BABY TO A BIG GIRL, I'LL ALWAYS BE
HERE FOR YOU.
& IT ISN'T NOTHING IN THIS WORLD, FOR YOU I
WOULDN'T DO.
SOME THINGS ARE BEYOND OUR
UNDERSTANDING, OUT OF OUR CONTROL.
LIFE IS GOOD BUT SOMETIMES IT CAN BE SO
COLD.
MY FEMALE MINI ME, I LOVE YOU SO MUCH.
I PRAY FOR THE DAY, THAT WE GET BACK IN
TOUCH.

LETTER TO MY DAUGHTER JAKIRA CUE
6-15

I REMEMBER SEEING YOU AT BIRTH I KNEW
YOU WERE MINE.
I ASKED YOUR MOTHER BUT SHE WAS
DENYING.
THEN I SEE YOU AGAIN AT 7 YEARS OLD.
SHE STILL DIDN'T LET IT BE KNOWN; THIS
WORLD IS COLD.
THEN WE REUNITED WHEN YOU WERE TEN.
& EVER SINCE THEN YOU BEEN IN MY LIFE
SINCE THEN.
WE CONNECTED LIKE I BEEN IN YOUR LIFE
SINCE BIRTH.
HAVING ALL MY KIDS, MAKE ME THE
PROUDEST DAD ON EARTH.
A SMART & BEAUTIFUL PRINCESS, DADDY'S
LITTLE GIRL.
& IT'S NOTHING I WOULDN'T DO, FOR YOU IN
THIS WORLD.
IT'S A PRICELESS MOMENT, EVERY TIME I'M
WITH MY KIDS.
& IF ANYONE TRY TO HARM YOU, I'LL HAVE TO
DO A BID.
THE YEARS I MISS I CAN'T MAKE UP, BUT I'M
HERE NOW.
IF YOU EVER NEED ME, JUST CALL, TO REACH
ME YOU KNOW HOW.
I LOVE YOU WITH ALL MY HEART, I'LL BE HERE
UNTIL THE END.
I'M HERE LIKE I'M A PART OF THE CULTURE &
NOT JUST A TREND.

PHASE II.   THE AWAKENING

HANDICAPPED BY HISTORY...

I'M SITTING HERE LEARNING THE LIES MY
TEACHER TOLD ME.
& THE UNTOLD STORIES, SO YOU CAN RESPECT
WHITE HISTORY.
THE SPANIARDS CAME WITH THE
REQUIREMENT WITH THE BIBLE IN HAND.
TO MAKE NATIVE AMERICANS CHRISTIANS, SO
THEY CAN STEAL THEY LAND.
THEY WERE LOOKING FOR THE GOLD,
WITHOUT A CARE FOR AN INDIAN SOUL.
ENSLAVING, MURDERING, & RAPING
EVERYONE FROM THE YOUNG TO THE OLD.
BUT THIS IS THE PART OF HISTORY THAT GO
UNTOLD.
TO MAKE CHRISTOPHER COLUMBUS LOOK LIKE
A HERO.
BUT IF THEY GAVE YOU ALL THE FACTS, HE
WOULD LOOK LIKE A ZERO.
PLUS, THE PILGRIMS WASN'T NO BETTER, THE
WAY THEY BEHAVE.
JUST TO SURVIVE IN THE NEW LAND, THEY
ROBBED THE INDIANS GRAVES.
THEY LEARN FROM THE NATIVES HOW TO
HUNT, GATHER, & PLANT CROPS.
THEN TURNED AROUND AND GAVE THEM
BLANKETS WITH DISEASES, THEN MASSACRED
THEM LIKE THEY WERE OP'S.

STOLE A WHOLE COUNTRY, SO AFRICA GOODS
WERE NO LONGER NEEDED FOR TRADE.
THE ONLY THING AFRICA HAD TO OFFER WERE
SLAVES, SOME WERE STOLEN, SOME HAD
PRICES THAT WERE PAID.
THEY BROUGHT AFRICANS IN & SHIPPED THE
INDIANS OUT.
& STILL TO THIS DAY FREEDOM, JUSTICE, &
EQUALITY WE ARE WITHOUT.

FROM SLAVE PATROL TO THE POLICE

NOTHING'S EVER CHANGED FROM SLAVE
PATROL TO THE POLICE.
WHITE PEOPLE THEY PROTECT & SERVE
MELANATED PEOPLE GET NO PEACE.
WITH THIS UNJUST JUSTICE SYSTEM, ALL YOU
SEE IS JUST US.
THEY USE TO PACK US ON THE SLAVE SHIPS,
NOW THEY PACK US ON THE PRISON BUS.
OVER PATROLLING OUR COMMUNITIES,
PREYING ON THE YOUNG BLACK MALE.
VIOLATING THE YOUNGSTERS' RIGHTS,
SETTING THEM UP IN LIFE TO FAIL.
YOU CAN'T TELL ME DRED SCOTT LAW ISN'T
STILL IN EFFECT.
WE PAY TAXES TOO, BUT THEY DON'T SERVE US
NOR PROTECT.
DRUGS & CRIMES EXIST ALSO IN WHITE
COMMUNITIES.

IF THEY PATROL THEM LIKE THE BLACK
NEIGHBORHOODS, THE RATIO YOU'D SEE.
EVERY BLACK MAN FIT THE DESCRIPTION OF
SOMEONE WHO JUST COMMITTED A FELON.
BLACK MAN BECOME A POLICE & TURN TO
SAMBO; CAN YOU IMAGINE WHAT HE TELLS
THEM.
ALL POLICE ISN'T BAD, BUT THE GOOD ONES
NEVER SPEAK UP.
THEY BE TOO BUSY EATING DOUGHNUTS,
SIPPING COFFEE OUT A CUP.
WHY IS MELANATED PEOPLE, THE ONLY ONES
TO GET ACCIDENTLY KILLED BY COPS.
FOX NEWS JUSTIFY EVERYTHING THEY DO,
THEY REALLY ARE THE OP'S.
THEN FLIP THE SCRIPT & MAKE IT LIKE THE
POLICE ARE VICTIMS OF CRIME.
THE REASON FOR THEIR ACTIONS, THEY
FEARED FOR THEY LIFE EVERY TIME.
SURRENDERING WITH OUR HANDS UP OR
RUNNING, BLACK PEOPLE STILL GET SHOT IN
THE BACK.
BUT SOON AS WE BUST BACK, THEY WANT TO
SAY IT'S A COWARDLY ACT.
WHITE PRIVILEGED & SUPREMACY WITH
BADGES IS ALL I SEE IN MY SIGHT.
FROM SLAVERY DAYS TO THE TWENTY FIRST
CENTURY, WILL STILL FIGHTING FOR OUR
RIGHTS

RACIST COWARDS WITH BADGES

TWO OFFICERS CONVICTED OF KILLING TWO
BLACK LIVES IN THE SAME WEEK IS HISTORY.
BUT THE POLICE TURNED AROUND & KILL
THREE MORE OF US IN THE SAME WEEK IS NO
MYSTERY.
THEY TRY TO JUSTIFY THEY MURDERS BY
BRINGING UP THE VICTIMS PAST.
INSTEAD OF THE CURRENT SITUATION, THAT
MADE THEM BLAST.
A WHITE PERSON THAT MASS MURDER THEY
NEVER FEAR, GET BROUGHT INTO CUSTODY
WITH NO HARM.
BUT THEY FEAR FOR THEY LIFE, WITH A BLACK
PERSON IN A TRAFFIC STOP UNARMED.
THEN JUSTIFY THEY ACTIONS TALKING ABOUT
FAMILY PROBLEMS & MENTAL HEALTH
CONDITION.
THEN USE FOX NEWS COVERAGE TO STIR UP
THE TENSION.
CAUGHT ON CAMERA DEAD WRONG, THE
POLICE NEVER DO WRONG IN THEIR EYES.
IF YOU ARE MELANATED YOU ARE
AUTOMATICALLY GUILTY, THE POLICE ARE
ALWAYS THE GOOD GUYS.
156 YEARS LATER WE STILL HAVE UNEQUAL
JUSTICE & NO PEACE.
WE CAN GO FIGHT IN A WAR FOR OUR
COUNTRY & COME HOME AND GET HARASS BY
THE POLICE.
WE SUPPOSED TO BE THE GREATEST NATION
ON EARTH, BUT DON'T RESPECT THE ORIGINAL

MAN.
THEY HATE US AS HUMANS SO MUCH, BUT OUR
CULTURE THEY ARE OUR BIGGEST FAN.
THEY WANT US TO PRAISE THEY GOD, BUT
THEIR ACTIONS OF THE DEVIL.
THEY SWEAR THEY ARE SO SUPERIOR TO US
BUT WANT GIVE US AN EQUAL LEVEL.
SLAVERY NEVER STOP, PRISON IS THE MODERN-
DAY PLANTATIONS.
SLAVERY IS MORE MENTAL NOW; THEY ARE
TRYING TO ENSLAVE THE MASSES OF OUR
NATION.
THE PEOPLE THAT RULE THE WORLD IS LESS
THAN 10 PERCENT.
WITH ENOUGH MONEY TO OWN A COUNTRY,
WHERE THE AVERAGE PERSON CAN BARELY
AFFORD TO PAY THEY RENT.
A BLACK MAN MUST SELL OUT HIS OWN PEOPLE
TO BE ACKNOWLEDGED & ACCEPTED.
BE ONE IN MILLIONS TO MAKE IT, & SWEAR
OUR RIGHTS AREN'T NEGLECTED
GIVE THEM A BADGE & A GUN & THEY CAN
LEGALLY HUNT US LIKE PREY.
& THEN WONDER WHY WE ARE STILL
SCREAMING FUCK THE POLICE TO THIS VERY
DAY.

FIGHT OR GO HOME

WE ORIGINATED IN THE MOTHERLAND, THE
FIRST HUMANS TO STEP FOOT ON THIS EARTH.
WE ARE KINGS & QUEENS, INTO SLAVERY
WASN'T OUR BIRTH.
WE WERE SOLD & STOLE, INTO THIS LIFE OF
MISERY.
& FOR SEVERAL GENERATIONS, WE ARE STILL
FIGHTING TO BE FREE.
WE GOT TO STAND FOR SOMETHING OR KEEP
FALLING FOR ANYTHING.
OR KEEP GETTING HOODWINKED &
BAMBOOZLED OVER & OVER AGAIN.
REPUBLICAN OR DEMOCRATS NEITHER OF
THESE PARTY'S CARED FOR US AS A PEOPLE.
THEY LABELED US ¾ OF A HUMAN BEING, WE
HAVE NEVER BEEN TREATED EQUAL.
THEY ONLY ACKNOWLEDGE US WHEN THEY
NEED US TO FIGHT IN THEIR WAR OR TO WIN
AN ELECTION.
THEN WHEN WE ARE MISTREATED, THEY ACT
DUMB & MUTE WHEN WE NEED, THEY
PROTECTION.
THEY TELL THE ATHLETES TO SHUT UP & BALL
THE PRISONERS CAN'T RUN THE PRISON.
NOT KNOWING THAT BLACK LIVES MATTER,
DON'T MAKE YOU A PATRICIAN.
THEY LOVE OUR CULTURE BUT HATE US AS A
PEOPLE.
WE ARE THE ORIGINATORS AND THEY ARE
REMAKES, WAIT FOR OUR SEQUEL.
WE NEED TO FIGHT FOR WHAT'S OURS HERE,

OR GO BACK HOME & REBUILD OUR NATION.
& CONTINUE THE VISION OF MARCUS GARVEY
& THE UNIVERSAL NEGRO IMPROVEMENT
ASSOCIATION

MELANATED WOMAN IS DEITY

NUBIAN QUEEN IS GOD, I AM JUST TRYING TO
MAKE IT BACK TO HEAVEN.
TWO NUMBER ONES TOGETHER TRYING TO
BECOME THREE, NOT JUST SIDE BY SIDE LIKE
ELEVEN.
THE MOTHER OF THIS EARTH, NO ONE CAME
BEFORE YOU.
THE ONLY MOTHER ON THIS EARTH, THAT CAN
CREATE A CHILD OF ALL HUES.
THE FIRST TO NURTURE THE CREATION OF
LIFE WITHIN HERSELF LIKE THE UNIVERSE.
SHE WILL MAKE YOU FEEL ALL MIGHTY, AFTER
YOU AND HER CONVERSE.
SHE IS THE FIRST TEACHER & MOTHER OF
CIVILIZATION.
WE NEED TO UPLIFT OUR GODDESSES & BRING
BACK A MATRIARCHAL NATION.
A NUBIAN GODDESS WILL HAVE YOU
HYPNOTIZED FROM HER BEAUTY & FINENESS.
BEING ON ONE ACCORD WITH HER, YOU CAN
CONQUER THE WORLD FROM HER DIVINENESS.
SO, ENTICING A MAN WILL DEDICATE HIS
WHOLE LIFE TO HER, EVEN IF IT CAUSES THE

DEATH OF HIM.
UNITED WE STAND, DIVIDED WE ARE OPPRESS
BY THEM.
AS MELANATED WARRIORS WE NEED TO
PROTECT OUR MOTHERS, SISTERS &
DAUGHTERS.
& MAKE THIS A PROMISE LAND AGAIN FOR OUR
PEOPLE, & NOT A OPEN SEASON FOR
SLAUGHTER.
TO ALL THE NUBIAN GODDESS OF THE WORLD,
I LOVE YOU & THANK YOU FOR LIFE.
& I PRAY TO THE ALL MOST HIGH ONE DAY I
CAN MAKE ONE MY WIFE

GRA'MA HOUSE

THERE'S NO AMOUNT OF MONEY I WOULDN'T
PAY TO REVISIT MY GRA'MA HOUSE AGAIN.
MY EARLIEST MEMORIES STARTED THERE, AS
MY LIFE BEGIN.
THE HONORABLE MR. ROY & MRS. DORIS
OWENS AKA MR. ROY & MRS. DOT.
THE PLACE OF MY MOST PRECIOUS MEMORIES
OF MY CHILDHOOD SPOT.
I MISS GRA'MA COOKING ALL 3 HOT MEALS.
BREAKFAST, LUNCH, DINNER, YOUR
GUARANTEED TO STAY FILL.
YOU ARE NOT GOING JUST SIT AROUND, SHE
GOING TO GIVE YOU A CHORE.
EITHER MOWING, RAKING, OR CLEANING THE
YARD, OR DOING THE DISHES OR SWEEPING
THE FLOOR.

GRA'MA & GRANDDADDY STAYED IN THE
FIELD, GROWING THEY OWN FRUITS & VEGS.
WHEN WE WERE BAD, WE HAD TO PICK THE
SWITCHES, GRA'MA WENT TO WORK ON OUR
LEGS.
PEOPLE SCARED TO PASS BY OUR HOUSE
BECAUSE THE DOGS WOULD CHASE THEM
AWAY.
MY FAVORITE DOG WAS BIG FOOT, WITH HER I
WISH I COULD GET ONE MORE DAY.
WHEN GRANDDADDY GRABBED HIS HAT AND
HIS KEYS WE'D RUN TO THE CAR.
TRYING TO GET IN THE FRONT SEAT, HOPING
WE WAS GOING FAR.
DO NOT TURN THE T.V. GRA'MA DIDN'T PLAY
ABOUT HER FAVORITE SHOWS.
WE COULDN'T WAIT UNTIL IT WAS A BASEBALL
GAME, SO GRANDDADDY COULD TAKE US IF HE
GOES.
I MISS EVERY SUNDAY HAVING TO GO TO
CHURCH & SUNDAY SCHOOL.
& THEN HAVING FAMILY OVER FOR SUNDAY
DINNERS, THEM DAYS WAS SO COOL.
WHAT I WOULDN'T GIVE TO VISIT GRA'MA
HOUSE ONE MORE TIME.
UNTIL WE MEET AGAIN IT IS SIMPLY GREAT
MEMORIES IN MY MIND.

HAPPY MOTHER'S DAY

SINCE MY DATE OF BIRTH, I WAS MOM PRIDE & JOY.
I HATED TO BE SEPARATED FROM MY MOM, I WAS A MOMMA'S BOY.
THE GREATEST MOM ALIVE IN MY EYES & PRESENCE.
SHE WAS ALWAYS THERE TO KEEP ME GROUNDED WHEN THINGS GOT TO TENSE.
I REMEMBER SHE WENT TO KANSAS, & LEFT US AT GRANDMA HOUSE, I CRIED ON THE FLOOR.
EVERY TIME SOMEONE CAME OVER, I WAS HOPING IT WAS HER, COMING THRU THE DOOR.
I REMEMBER GOING TO THE STORE BEGGING FOR TOYS, SAYING MOM IF YOU GET ME THIS, I WANT ASK FOR NOTHING ELSE.
THEN THE NEXT TRIP TO THE STORE, I WAS BEGGING FOR SOMETHING ELSE.
MOM KEEP ME FRESH WITH THE NEW KICKS.
I GOT OLDER, I HAD TO STAY FLY WITH THE NEW KICKS.
I STARTED GETTING IN TROUBLE WHEN I WAS A TEEN.
MY MOM WAS ALWAYS THERE THROUGHOUT ANYTHING.
WHEN I GOT GROWN, WE HAD OUR UPS & DOWN.
BUT THAT'S LIFE & NOTHING COULD STOP ME FROM COMING AROUND.
MY MOM WAS ALWAYS STRONG & AMBITIOUS, I GET IT FROM YOU.

I WOULD BE HAPPY IF MY WIFE BE 25% OF YOU.
TO HAVE OUR FAMILY TOGETHER WOULD BE
MY GREATEST DAY.
I LOVE YOU SO MUCH MOM, HAPPY MOTHER'S
DAY.

MY FIVE HEARTBEATS

I LOVE MY KIDS SO MUCH, THEY ARE ALL THAT
I'M LIVING FOR.
I WAS SURPRISED WHEN I HAD A NEW EDITION
ADDED TO MY FANTASTIC FOUR.
IT ALL STARTED WITH THE DAYS OF ME &
LITTLE E.
MY FIRST BORN, AN UPGRADED VERSION OF
ME.
THEN I HAD MY SECOND BORN JALEB MY
LITTLE TWIN.
HE SO HUMBLE & RIGHTEOUS, I SWEAR HE
NEVER EVER SIN.
& THEN CAME MY FIRST-BORN DAUGHTER
JANAYA.
SHE BECAME A ELEMENT TO MY WORLD, LIKE
EARTH WIND, & FIRE.
THEN I HAD MY PRINCESS KAMARIA, FEMALE
VERSION OF ME.
ANYTHING IN THIS WORLD, I KNOW SHE
COULD BE.
LAST BUT NOT LESS, CAME JA'KIRA MY BABY
GIRL.

A FUTURE QUEEN THAT'S GOING TO SHINE
LIKE A PEARL.
THESE ARE THE WONDERS OF MY WORLD, THE
MAKINGS OF ME.
THEY ARE ALL I'M LIVING FOR; WITHOUT THEM
I DON'T KNOW WHO I'D BE.
I WISH I COULD REWIND THE DAYS WHEN THEY
WERE JUST LITTLE KIDS IN MY ARMS.
GETTING THEM READY FOR SCHOOL AFTER
BEING WOKE UP BY THE ALARM.
GOING SHOPPING TO THE MALL, OR
SOMEWHERE OUT TO EAT.
TAKING FAMILY PICTURES, THEM DAYS WAS SO
SWEET.
NOW THEY ARE IN THEIR TEENS OR ALL
GROWN UP TO BE YOUNG ADULTS.
MUCH LOVE TO THEIR MOTHERS, WHAT WE
MADE WERE AWESOME RESULTS.
DADDY WILL ALWAYS LOVE YOU EVEN AFTER
THE DAY I DIE.
YOU ALL ARE SPITTING IMAGINES OF ME; I
COULD NEVER DENY.

NO WORDS CAN DESCRIBE THE PAIN. BUT I'M
KNOW YOU TRANSCENDING TO BE AN ANGEL
UP IN HEAVEN. MY LAST
WORDS I TOLD YOU, WAS I LOVE YA'LL ON THE
PHONE THREE WAY WITH OUR SON EDWIN
BROOKS.

SHON SHON REST IN PEACE.

I'D NEVER FORGET THE FIRST TIME WE'D MEET.
I WAS GETTING OUT OF SCHOOL, WALKING
DOWN VERDELL STREET.
I WAS TOLD THAT YOU LIKED ME BY OUR
LITTLE SISTER PAM.
I WAS SCARED TO TALK TO YOU AS SHY AS I AM.
WHEN WE BEGIN TO TALK, WE WERE
INSEPARABLE.
WE HAD OUR UPS AND DOWNS, BUT I'D NEVER
LET YOU GO.
MY FIRST TRUE LOVE, MOTHER OF MY FIRST-
BORN SON.
HE HAS GROWN TO BE A YOUNG BRIGHT MAN,
THAT SHINE LIKE THE SUN.
I'D NEVER IMAGINE THE DAY, THAT I WOULD
HEAR THIS SAD NEWS.
I AM SITTING HERE REMINISCING, SAD & BLUE.
OUR LAST CONVERSATION WAS ON THE
PHONE, 3 WAY WITH OUR SON.
YOU WROTE A LETTER FOR ME; I'LL NEVER
FORGET WHAT YOU DONE.
I HAD YOU IN MY PRAYS, & I WILL KEEP YOU IN
MY PRAYS.
MY LOVE IS ETERNAL, I'LL ALWAYS CARE.
YOU WERE A LOVING GREAT PERSON, WITH A
BIG HEART.
IF I COULD TURN BACK THE HANDS OF TIME,
I'D HIT RESTART.
I'LL BE HERE FOR OUR SON TILL THE DAY THAT
I DECEASE.
SHONDA PEDA CORD FILER FOREVER REST IN
PEACE

GENESIS JOSEPH

THEY LOVE YOU, THEY HATE YOU, BECAUSE
YOU AMELIORATE.
I HAD A DREAM THEY BE BEHIND ME AS I
NAVIGATE.
I'D BE THE GREAT ONE AND THEY'D ALL BOW
DOWN.
BUT THEY RATHER SEE ME DEAD, BEFORE IT
ALL GO DOWN.
THEY SET ME UP & SOLD ME OUT, HAD ME
TOOK AWAY.
I RISE TO THE TOP, EVERYWHERE I STAY.
THEY LIED TO MY PEOPLE AND SAID I WAS
DEAD AND GONE.
BUT I'M IN A FOREIGN PLACE, LIVING LIKE THIS
IS WHERE I BELONG.
WITH SUCCESS COMES JEALOUSY, AND A
WHOLE LOT OF HATE.
A ENVIOUS PERSON WILL ALWAYS TRY TO SEAL
YOUR FATE.
I GET LIED ON AGAIN, THEN I GO TO JAIL.
THE LIMITS THEY GO TOO, TO TRY TO SEE ME
FAIL.
I'M HIGHLY FAVORED AND BLESS, THE ALL-
LOVES ME.
OF COURSE, I'M BACK ON TOP WHEN I GET
FREE.
THE DEVIL USES THEM UP, NOW THEIR SERVICE
IS NO LONGER NEEDED.
WHILE THEY DECLINE, I EXCEEDED.
IT'S THE MOST HIGH, ALL IN ME FOR ME NOT
TO TURN MY BACK.

I FEED THEM WITH A LONG HANDLE SPOON
BEFORE I TAKE THEM BACK.
THE TRUTH COMES OUT BECAUSE TIME TELL IT
ALL.
BECAUSE THE GOD IN ME, WE LIVE HAPPILY
AFTER ALL

CELIBACY

IN STILLNESS I DWELL, UNTOUCHED, PURE,
I'M SO FOCUSED, I CAN'T SEE THE ALLURE.
NO PASSIONS WILD, MY HEART SECURE.
BEING MARRIED, WILL BE MY NEXT TIME I
ASSURE.

EMBRACING SOLITUDE, A SACRED SPACE,
SHE HAS TO BE HEAVEN SENT, I REFUSE TO
CHASE.
CHASTE FOREVER, MY SPIRIT'S GRACE.
I'M TAKING MY TIME, MOVING AT MY OWN
PACE.

CELIBATE FOR ALMOST 3 YEARS NOW.
MOST PEOPLE IS THINKING HOW.
IT'S ALL IN THE MIND, WHAT YOU ALLOW.
TO PROCEED, WE GONE NEED A VOW.

UNLOCKING MYSTERIES, FINDING SOLACE
DEEP,
MY NEXT WILL BE AFTER A BROOM LEAP.
BEING COMMITTED, NO TIME TO CREEP.
CELIBACY'S GIFT, MY SOUL TO KEEP.

RESURRECTED...

YOU PEASANTS WANTED TO SEE ME DOWN,
BUT YOU JUST MADE ME GREATER.
I THOUGHT JESUS WAS LOVE & YOU LOVE JESUS
SO MUCH, THEN HOW ARE YOU A HATER.
I KNOW THE SUN'S GOD & I'M GOD'S SON, SO
YOU KNOW I'M GOING TO SHINE.
YES, I'M ENLIGHTEN & I OVERSTAND YOU, BUT
YOU GOING TO RESPECT MY MIND.
FIRST, I WAS OVERHEATED, NOT KNOWING
GOD'S PLAN.
I LAID LO LIKE SHAWTY BECAUSE I KNOW THAT
I'M THE MAN.
& THEY KNOW I WAS GOING TO RETURN LIKE
CHRIST.
GOOD TIME WITH BAD PEOPLE, I HAD TO
SACRIFICE.
NO THIS ISN'T BLASPHEMY; THIS IS THE MOST
HIGH SPEAKING THRU ME.
THE LORD KNOW MY HEART, I AM WHO I AM
HAVE THE KEY.
DO NOT BE CONFORMED TO THIS WORLD, BUT
BE TRANSFORMED BY THE RENEWAL OF YOUR
MIND.
IF THE TRUTH YOU SEEK, THE TRUTH YOU
SHALL FIND.
I'M SO HUMBLE & AT PEACE, I COULDN'T GET
UPSET IF I TRIED TOO.
FIRST THE TRUTH WILL PISS YOU OFF, BUT
THEN IT SET YOU FREE, IF YOU DIDN'T KNEW.
NOW MY APPEARANCE IS LIKE LIGHTENING &
MY CLOTHING IS WHITE AS SNOW.

LOOK LIKE I'VE RISEN FROM THE DEAD, GO
TELL MY BROTHERS TO GO...

LOST SOULS

IN SHADOWS LOST, FORGOTTEN SOULS YEARN
FOR LIGHT,
THEY CAN BE RIGHT UP UNDER THE SUN, AND
WOULDN'T BE BRIGHT.
DEVIOUS ACTIONS CONSTANTLY COMMITTED
OUT OF SPITE.
EVOLVING SEEMS TO BE THEIR BIGGEST
FRIGHT.
SEEKING REDEMPTION AND CONSOLATION
UNTOLD,
CAN'T THINK FOR THEMSELVES, THEY HAVE TO
BE TOLD.
THERE'S NO MENDING THE FRAGMENTS OF
THEIR SOULS.
A WASTE OF TIME, AIR, AND SPACE, WITH NO
GOALS.
BUT IN THIS ABYSS, HOPE SEEMS SO FAR AWAY,
NO FUTURE PLANS, ONLY LIVING FOR TODAY.
LOST SOULS WANDER, THEIR SPIRITS IN
DISARRAY.
NEVER SEEM TO BE, WHO THEY DISPLAY.
CURSED IS THE ATMOSPHERE THEY ROAM,
YOU'D SWEAR, SATAN SITTING BEHIND A
CONTROL BOARD IN THEIR DOME.
HATE AND IGNORANCE IS EMBEDDED IN
THEIR CHROMOSOMES.
NO GLIMMER OF HOPE, SUFFERING FROM
WILLIE LYNCH SYNDROME.

WISHING ON MY DOWNFALL

ENVIOUS EYES CAST JEALOUS SPELLS,
IF IT'S LIKE THIS ON EARTH, CAN YOU IMAGINE
HELL.
WISHING MY DOWNFALL THEY FORETELL.
THEN LOOK SO DISGUSTED, AS I EXCEL.
BUT PERSEVERANCE FUELS MY FIRE,
I AM A PRODUCT OF THE ALL MOST HIGHER.
HIGHER AND HIGHER I ASPIRE.
IN DISBELIEF OF REALITY, SO THEY BECOME
LIARS.
IN THEIR ENVY THEY FAIL TO SEE,
THE STRENGTH AND RESILIENCE, THAT SETS
ME FREE.
THE SAME ENERGY THEY USING TO HATE,
THEY CAN PURSUE TO BE.
IT MUST BE IN THEIR DNA, TO HATE AND ENVY.
THEIR WISHES CRUMBLE, WITH ALL THE
USELESS SCHEMES,
THEIR IN DENIAL, TO ACKNOWLEDGE I AM
SUPREME.
I CAN'T SETTLE FOR BEING STANDARD, I
THRIVE TO BE EXTREME.
WHILE I CONTINUE TO RISE, I DESTROY THEIR
DREAMS.

MY LOVE ONE'S

I TRULY APPRECIATE EVERYONE WHO BEEN
HERE FOR ME, THROUGH THIS DOWN TIME.
WHEN I GET FREE, BACK TO THE TOP IS WHERE
I'M GOING TO CLIMB.
SPIRITUALLY AND MORALLY UPGRADED,
BETTER THAN EVER.
SOME PEOPLE IN MY LIFE, COMPLETELY FROM I
HAD TO SEVER.
JUST ANOTHER LIFE LESSON, WE LIVE AND WE
LEARN.
I'M NO LONGER REBUILDING BRIDGES, SO
THEY CAN CONTINUE TO BURN.
THE PEOPLE THAT STOOD UP & RODE FOR ME, I
TRULY LOVE YOU ALL.
ONLY DEATH CAN STOP ME, OR BE THE NEXT
REASON I FALL.
LOVE, PEACE, AND HAPPINESS, IS ALL I PURSUE.
& BEING GREAT, IS WHAT I'M GONNA
CONTINUE TO DO.
SOME PEOPLE IS JUST A WASTE OF TIME, NO
MATTER WHAT YOU DO YOU CAN'T HELP THEM.
I'M LIVING PROOF, I'M THE TRUTH, THIS IS
REALISM.
THE BATTLE'S NOT MINE, IT'S THE ALL MOST
HIGH.
& I'M GONNA GIVE IT MY ALL, UNTIL I LIVE IN
THE SKY.
MY DESTINY IS TO PAY YOU ALL BACK, BEFORE
IT'S ALL DONE.
EVEN THOUGH YOUR DEEDS ARE PRICELESS,
I'M TRULY THANKFUL FOR MY LOVE ONES.

PHASE III THE TRANSITION

LIFE'S 360

WHAT'S GOES AROUND, SURELY COMES BACK
AROUND.
LIKE THE EARTH ROTATION, GOING ROUND
AND ROUND.
BE CAREFUL OF THE ENERGY YOU PUT OUT, IN
THE ATMOSPHERE.
THE SAME SPIRIT MIGHT MAKE YOU FROWN,
THAT ONCE MADE YOU CHEER.
EVERY INDIVIDUAL LIFE'S JOURNEY
DIFFERENT, WE ALL LIVE AND WE LEARN.
TRY TO BETTER THE PEOPLE AROUND YOU,
ENLIGHTEN TO WHOM MAY CONCERN.
SOME DAYS ARE BETTER THAN OTHERS, BUT
NEVER GIVE UP.
NEVER FORGET THE DAYS YOU WERE DOWN,
WHEN YOU GET UP.
ONLY A FOOL WILL CONTINUE THE SAME
ACTIONS, LOOKING FOR DIFFERENT RESULTS.
NEVER WORRY ABOUT WHAT THE NEXT
PERSON THINK, BE MOTIVATED BY INSULTS.
BE ABLE TO SHOW PEOPLE, BETTER THAN YOU
CAN TELL.
ALWAYS YOUR ALL YOU HAVE TO GIVE, NEVER
MAKE IT AN OPTION TO FAIL.
LIVE TO IMPRESS THE ALL MOST HIGH, NEVER
LIVE TO IMPRESS MAN.
YOU'LL ALWAYS BE SATISFIED, WHEN YOU DO
THE BEST YOU CAN.

THE ONES THAT ONCE HATED YOU, WILL SOON
GAIN TO LOVE YOU.
BESIDE THE ALL MOST HIGH, PUT NO MAN
ABOVE YOU.

NEGATIVE ENERGY

PROTECT YOUR VISION, HEARING, AND
BEWARE OF THE COMPANY YOU KEEP.
SOME NEGATIVE ENERGY IS STRAIGHT
FORWARD IMPACTFUL, SOME SLOWLY BUT
SURELY CREEP.
IT'S MORE CONTAGIOUS THAN COVID-19, SO BE
CAUTIOUS AND SAFE.
YOUR PERSONAL SPACE IS SCARED, YOU
SHOULD GUARD IT LIKE A SAFE.
PROTECT YOUR VIBE, BY ANY MEANS
NECESSARY.
SOME PEOPLE GOALS ARE TO MAKE YOU
MISERABLE, AND SEND YOU TO A CEMETERY.
THAT'S HOW THEY MAKE THEY LOW LIFE FEEL
HIGH.
NO MATTER HOW MUCH LOVE YOU SHOW TO
THEM, THEY'LL CONTINUOUSLY TRY.
THEY SAY HATE MOTIVATE, BUT AFTER A
WHILE IT IRRITATE.
LIFE IS TOO SHORT, DON'T LET A DEVIL
DETOUR YOUR FATE.
DO NOT CONFORM TO THE PATTERN OF THIS
WORLD, BUT BE TRANSFORMED BY THE
RENEWING OF YOUR MIND.

BEING CAUGHT UP IN THESE WORLDLY WAYS,
WILL HAVE YOU DUMB, DEAF, AND BLIND.
KEEP YOUR SPIRITS HIGH, BECAUSE YOU ARE
VULNERABLE WHEN YOU ARE STRESSED AND
DEPRESSED.
THE ALL MOST HIGH IS WHO YOU SHOULD BE
LIVING TO IMPRESS
NOBODIES PERFECT, LIVE AND LEARN, BE THE
BEST PERSON YOU CAN BE.
TRY YOUR BEST TO AVOID, AND DON'T NOT
OUTPUT NEGATIVE ENERGY.

INAPPROPRIATE BEHAVIOR

BLACK PEOPLE CAUSE A RUCKUS WHEN THEY
GET CALLED A N!66@, BUT NOT WHEN THEY
TREATED LIKE ONE.
IF WE TOOK HAVING EQUAL RIGHTS & NATION
BUILDING MORE SERIOUS THAN CLUBBING,
TURNING UP, OR HAVING MORE
FUN.
WE'D BE A RACE TO BE RESPECTED, & TOOK
MORE SERIOUSLY.
INSTEAD, WE TEAM LIGHT SKIN VERSUS DARK
SKIN, LOOKING DELIRIOUS.
A THREAT TO NOBODY BUT OUR OWN PEOPLE.
THINKING MARCHING & PROTESTING GOING
TO MAKE US EQUAL.
GET BAMBOOZLED EVERY TIME WE VOTE, TO
GET NO RESULTS.

WE ARE GETTING TAXATION WITH NO
REPRESENTATION, THAT'S AN INSULT.
BLACK MEDIA, RADIO TALK SHOWS,
NEWSPAPERS, ETCETERA ONLY HUMILIATE OUR
RACE.
MAJORITY OF THEIR PROGRAMS THEY DISCUSS,
GOSSIP, CRIMES, AND IGNORANCE TO
DISGRACE OUR RACE.
WE GET A LITTLE MONEY NOW, WE TOO GOOD
TO LIVE IN THE HOOD.
INSTEAD OF INVESTING OUR MONEY AND
BUILDING UP OUR OWN NEIGHBORHOOD.
WE LOVE TO LET OTHER PEOPLE GET RICH OFF
US, BUT WANT SUPPORT EACH OTHER.
BLACK BUSINESS DAMN NEAR HAVE TO BEG TO
GET SUPPORT, FROM THEY OWN SISTERS &
BROTHERS.
THEN THEY WANT A DISCOUNT WITH A BLACK
BUSINESS, BUT WILL TIP FOREIGNERS THAT
NEVER SPEND A DIME BACK.
BABY DADDIES & BABY MOMMA IS THE NORM,
NOW WE NEED TO GET OUR FAMILIES BACK ON
TRACK.
MOST OF US DON'T KNOW OUR OWN TRUE
HISTORY.
THEY SCHOOLS TAUGHT US THAT IT STARTED
WITH SLAVERY.
IGNORANCE IN MUSIC, MOVIES & T.V. SHOWS IS
THE MODERN-DAY BLACKFACE.
SPENDING MONEY WITH PEOPLE THAT DON'T
LIKE YOU, AND GET MAD WHEN THEY DON'T
WANT YOU IN THEY PLACE.
DOING STUPID CRIMES AND KILLING EACH
OTHER FOR LITTLE OR NOTHING TO KEEP

PRISON FILLED.
BUT IF A BLACK INVESTS IN A PRISON, HE'S THE
ONE THAT'S ILL.
NOT TO MENTION THE ONE'S THAT WORK
THERE.
WE ARE OUR OWN ENEMY, THAT'S WHY IT'LL
NEVER BE FAIR.

MOTHER OF MY CHILDREN

THE BLACK WOMAN IS GODDESS & QUEENS, I
THANK YOU FOR BIRTHING MY CHILDREN.
THANKS FOR RAISING MY SEEDS TO BE GOD &
GODDESS, IN THIS LIFE FULL OF SIN.
WE MADE A LOVE CHILD, THAT'S GOD 'S PLAN
NO MISTAKE.
TO KEEP THEM HAPPY & SATISFIED, YOU GAVE
IT ALL THAT IT TAKES.
THE GREAT MOTHERS OF MY CHILDREN,
ALWAYS MADE A WAY.
I CRIED FOR YOU LIKE JODECI, & WISH THAT
YOU'D STAY.
WE CAN'T TURN BACK THE HANDS OF TIME,
BUT WE CAN MAKE BETTER THE FUTURE &
PRESENT.
THE GREATEST GIFT IN MY LIFE, IS MY
CHILDREN PRESENCE.
BEAUTIFUL & INTELLIGENT VERSION OF US,
BOUND TO BE SUCCESSFUL IN LIFE.
MY WORST DECISION WAS NOT MAKING YOU,
MY WIFE.

EVEN THOUGH WE MADE THE BEST OUT OF
HAVING KIDS OUT OF WEDLOCK.
I CAN NEVER PAY YOU BACK FROM BIRTHING
OUR PRICELESS STOCK.
THROUGH THE UPS & DOWNS I ALWAYS HAD
LOVE.
IF WE WERE ON ONE ACCORD, WE'D BE SO FAR
ABOVE.
SINCE MY KID WERE IN YOUR WOMB, AND
EVERY DAY SINCE THEY BEEN IN MY PRAYERS.
ALL I HEAR IS, THEY LOOK JUST LIKE ME FROM
ALL OF THE YEA-SAYERS.
I KNOW THEY WILL CARRY ON OUR LEGACY;
THEY ARE DESTINING TO BE.
FOR THE REST OF MY LIVING DAYS, YOU CAN
COUNT ON ME.
I TRULY THANK YOU FROM THE BOTTOM OF
MY HEART, ALL OF MY LOVE I'M SENDING.
WE CAN'T UNDO THE PAST BUT WE CAN MAKE
THIS A HAPPY ENDING.

BABY MOMMA

MOST OF THESE BROADS DON'T WANT TO BE
WIVES, THEY WANT TO BE BABY MOMMAS.
DON'T KNOW HOW TO PROSPER OR LIVE IN
PEACE, SO THEY KEEP UP THE DRAMA.
THEY'LL CREATE A PROBLEM, IF YOU DON'T
HAVE NONE.
CALL YOU A DEAD BEAT, WHILE KEEPING YOU
AWAY FROM YOUR DAUGHTER & SON.

NEVER SATISFIED IT'S ALWAYS AN ISSUE.
BLOCK YOU ON SOCIAL MEDIA, BUT THEN
MAKE POST TO DISS YOU.
DON'T WANT YOUR KIDS AROUND YOUR NEW
GIRL, BUT KEEP THEM AROUND ALL THEY
DUDES.
DON'T HAVE NO RESPECT FOR THEMSELVES,
ALWAYS ACTING IGNORANT & RUDE.
ALL ABOUT THEMSELVES, & DON'T CARE
ABOUT NOBODY.
THAT'S WHY THEY ALWAYS SINGLE, CAN'T
KEEP NOBODY.
PUTTING YOUR MAN BEFORE YOUR KIDS, AND
STILL CAN'T KEEP ONE.
THINKING YOU HAVE ALL THE SENSE IN THE
WORLD, BUT REALLY DON'T HAVE NONE.
THEY HATE TO SEE YOU LIVING HAPPY &
GOOD, THEY'LL FILE A FALSE REPORT.
HAVE YOU LOCKED UP FOR A LIE, GOING BACK
AND FORTH TO COURT.
SO PETTY THAT EVEN THOUGH YOU TAKE
CARE OF YOUR KIDS, THEY STILL PUT YOU ON
CHILD SUPPORT.
EVEN THOUGH YOU LOVE YOUR KID, BUT HER
YOU WISH SHE HAD AN ABORT.
GENERATION AFTER GENERATION ON
SECTION 8 & FOOD STAMPS A BROKE HO
HUSTLE.
BE TOOK WELL TAKEN CARE OF, AND STILL
KNOCK HER OWN DAMN HUSTLE.
HAVE SEVERAL BABY DADDIES, BUT ALL
N!66@'$ AIN'T
NEVER LOOK IN THE MIRROR TO SEE WHO'S
THE CAUSE OF IT.

MISERY LOVE COMPANY AND YOU ALWAYS
HAVING A PITY PARTY.
HAVE ALL THE SENSE IN THE WORLD, WHEN IT
COMES TO CAUSING DRAMA, BUT WHEN IT
COMES TO DOING RIGHT YOU
AREN'T A SMARTY.
IT'S A CONFUSING FEELING WHEN YOU LOVE
YOUR CHILD AND HATE THEY MOTHER.
THEY OWN FAMILY KNOW THEY NOT SH!T,
FROM THEIR GRANDPARENTS TO THEIR
COUSINS & BROTHER.
IT'S SAD THAT MINUTES OF PLEASURE, CAN
CAUSE YOU YEARS OF PAIN.
IT'S ALMOST IMPOSSIBLE TO DEAL WITH SO
MUCH DRAMA, AND STILL REMAIN SANE.

ジャナヤさんのアート

IN COLORS BOLD, HER SPIRIT THRIVES,
AT HER BIRTH, A STAR ARRIVES.
BRUSHSTROKES DANCE, STORIES UNFOLD,
I WAS BLESS TO SEE GREATNESS BEING MOLD.
SPLASHED ON CANVAS, HER DREAMS ARISE,
WITNESSING GREATNESS, TIME SURELY FLIES.

CREATING ART, TOO PRICELESS TO BE
SOLD.
A MASTERPIECE, HER HEART'S TRUE GOLD.
VIBRANT VISIONS SPARKLE AND DELIGHT,
A MIRACLE BEING MADE EVERY TIME SHE
WRITE.
A WINDOW TO HER SOUL'S PURE LIGHT,

NATURALLY ILLUMINATED, SHE SHINE SO
BRIGHT.
GREATNESS IN THE FLESH, WORLD BEHOLD.
HER TALENT TOO AWESOME TO WITHHOLD.
BRINGING THE HEAT, TO THIS DIMENSION
THAT'S COLD.
PROUDLY SHE PAINTS HER WORLD, THAT'S
UNTOLD

MELANATED BARBIE

IN HER EYES, BRILLIANCE BRIGHTLY GLEAMS,
SEE CAME TO REALITY, FROM A DREAM.
A SOULFUL WONDER, KNOWLEDGE STREAMS.
IT'S IN HER ESSENCE AND DNA, TO BE
SUPREME.
WITH EACH WORD SHE SPEAKS, THE WORLD
EXPANDS,
DESTINE TO BE, AND SHE UNDERSTANDS.
A WISE MIND LIES WITHIN HER GENTLE HANDS.
NOTHING LIFE THROWS AT HER, SHE CAN'T
WITHSTAND.
HER BEAUTY, LIKE A BLOSSOMING FLOWER,
BEING INTELLIGENT, GIVES HER MORE POWER.
RADIATES GRACE, EACH PASSING HOUR.
SHE MAKES LIFE SWEET, WHEN IT'S SO SOUR.
HER BRILLIANCE AND BEAUTY, A PERFECT
BLEND,
IN A LEAGUE OF HER OWN, NO ONE CAN
CONTEND.
FROM GREATNESS, SHE HAS DESCEND.
A DAUGHTER UNMATCHED, A LOVE WITHOUT
END.

FROM A PRINCESS TO A QUEEN

FROM PRINCESS TO QUEEN, THE CROWN
ASCENDS,
BEING A PROUD FATHER, I MUST COMMEND.
A JOURNEY IN GRACE, WHERE STRENGTH
TRANSCENDS.
THE PRESENTS OF GREATNESS, IS EVERYWHERE
SHE ATTENDS.
WITH ELEGANCE AND WISDOM, HER REIGN
UNFOLDS,
HER ILLUMINATING MELANIN, WORTH MORE
THAN GOLD.
A REGAL HEART, STEADFAST AND BOLD.
HER PRESENCE IN THE ATMOSPHERE, YOU
MUST BEHOLD.
THROUGH TRIALS FACED, A SOVEREIGN'S
EMBRACE.
A DEMEANOR OF ELEGANCE AND GRACE.
A LEGACY OF POWER, ETCHED IN TIME'S
CHASE.
LAST BORN, DESTINE TO BE THE ACE.
FROM PRINCESS TO QUEEN, A CROWN PASSED
ON,
LIFE ISN'T A SPRINT, IT'S A MARATHON.
GREATNESS TO TRANSCEND FOR EONS.
AN HEIR TO THE THRONE, HER DESTINY
DAWNED.
SUN SON.

WHEN MY POSITIVE VIBRATIONS GET LOW, I
CLOSE MY EYES & PRAY.
WHEN YOU DOING GOOD, & GOOD AT HEART,

THEY LOOK AT YOU AS PREY.
THEY MAKE YOU BECOME THAT MAN, WHEN
THEY SEE YOU, AT MOST FEAR.
I'M LIKE NO OTHER, I'M FROM A DIFFERENT
ATMOSPHERE.
STAND FOR SOMETHING OR FALL FOR
ANYTHING, NEVER SELL YOUR SOUL.
I'M ALWAYS FLY, SUPER CLEAN FROM HAT TO
SOLE.
SO ICEY, COMING DOWN HITTING HARD AS
HELL.
WHEN I TOUCH DOWN, I'M GOING TO CAUSE
HELL.
I'M SO RIGHTEOUS, I CAN DO IT WITHOUT A SIN.

TOO TURNT, I REPLY TO A MESSAGE AND
FORGET TO PUSH SEND.
THIS IS MY REAL LIFE, THIS IS NOT NO FAIRY
TALE.
I HAD PLENTY KISSES, BUT I'D NEVER TELL.
I'M HEADED IN A NEW DIRECTION; THIS IS MY
PAST STORY.
THIS MY REAL-LIFE TESTIMONY, I PREACH IT
LIKE A PASTOR.
ME I'LL INNOVATE, INFLUENCE, ENLIGHTEN, &
BLESS YOU.
BEFORE I DOWN, MISGUIDE, DETOUR, OR LESS
YOU.
WHEN I FEEL IT IN MY SPIRIT, I PICK UP MY PEN
& WRITE.
IT'S A WASTE OF TIME TO DO IT WRONG, TAKE
YOUR TIME DO IT RIGHT.

RECONSTRUCTION.

THE MOST HIGH MADE ME TO AWESOME, TO
PUT AN END TO ME LIKE THIS.
I'VE BEEN STRIPPED OF EVERYTHING LIKE JOB,
ALL I HAVE LEFT IS THIS BLACK FIST.
AND THAT'S POWER, MADE IN THE IMAGE OF
GOD, & THAT'S WHAT I BECAME.
I'M IN CONTROL OF MY OWN DESTINY, IF I FAIL,
I AM TO BLAME.
I REFUSE TO LET THESE WHITE DEVILS &
BOURGEOIS NEGROES' PUT AN END TO ME.
I'M HATED FOR BEING ENLIGHTEN & GOOD
HEARTED, THAT'S A BAD FEELING TO BE.

IT'S A HARD FEELING WHEN YOU CAN'T TRUST
YOUR OWN PEOPLE.
WE ARE WARRING AMONGST OURSELVES,
WHEN WE SHOULD BE FIGHTING FOR RIGHTS
TO BE EQUAL.
THEY HATE TO SEE A BROTHER INTELLIGENT
OR LIVING BETTER THAN THEM.
THEY RATHER TRY TO DESTROY, INSTEAD OF
BEING INSPIRED BY HIM.
I'M ONLY GOING TO GET GREATER; GOD ISN'T
FINISHED WITH ME YET.
I'M AGAINST ALL ODDS FROM THE SYSTEM
THAT'S BEEN SET.
I'M IN TUNE WITH NATURE, ALIGNED WITH THE
STARS.
I AM UNLIKE THESE BEINGS, I HAD TO
DESCEND FROM MARS.
I'M JUST UPGRADING MYSELF, AWAITING MY

Cible

RETURN.
SIGN SINCERELY; TO WHOM THIS MAY CONCERN.

WASTING TIME SHOULD BE A SIN

WASTING TIME, SHOULD BE A SIN PROFOUND.
ONLY POSITIVE AND PRODUCTIVE PEOPLE, I LIKE TO BE SURROUND.
WHY LET PRECIOUS MOMENTS BE NON-ASTOUND?
I'M AN INTROVERT, THAT'S MORE PRODUCTIVE WHEN NO ONE IS AROUND.
IN MINUTES LOST, FORTUNES COULD BE FOREGONE.
I CAN DEAL WITH THE CONSEQUENCES, IF I'M THE REASON I NEVER WON.
LIFE'S ESSENCE SLIPS, AND IT'S FOREVER GONE.
BE PRODUCTIVE EVERYDAY, FROM NOW TO THEREON.
EACH BREATH IS A GIFT, EACH HEARTBEAT IS TRUE.
WASTING YOURS OR ANYONE'S TIME, YOU SHOULD NEVER DO.
EMBRACE EACH SECOND, BEFORE IT'S OVER WITH & THROUGH.
WAKING UP EVERYDAY, IS A BEGINNING THAT'S NEW.
FOR TIME'S EMBRACE, IS THE KEY TO FIND.
I'LL NEVER WASTE YOURS, PLEASE DON'T WASTE MINE.
HAVING ALL THE EXPENSIVE MATERIALISTIC ITEMS, MAKE YOU GO BLIND.

THE JOYS AND GOOD DEEDS, ARE THE MOST
IMPORTANT THINGS WE LEAVE BEHIND.

Convert.

I'm thinking of converting to Islam,
Christianity is the Indo-Europeans, &
their conquered people
Religion.
My brother Abe tried to been get me
to convert, & I should have been
made the decision.
Jesus was Muslim, most people don't
know that.
Because schools & churches give you
alternative facts.
Muslim is a brotherhood not based
on color or race.
While Sunday is the most segregated
day, & churches the most segregated
place.
Unless it's football season.
American's peacefully come together
for sports & entertainment, but no

other reason.
It's been over 400 years & we still
have the same racism problems.
We can build satellites, rockets, &
spaceships but can't solve them.
We still have the same issues Marcus
Garvey & Malcolm X was stressing.
Almost a century later, they haven't
seemed to lessing.
Just upgraded in a new system.
We still have bourgeoisie negro's
acting like they represent us, but
really speak for them.
They tell us we can & tell us to hope.
No party represent us, but tell us to
vote.
I want to be known for who I Am
not what I Am.
And that's the original man made in
the image of The All, Allah, I Am.

Better World.

I came a long way, but yet & still I got so far to go.
Should I just chill or go for what I know.
I want to make my impact on the world, fulfill my destiny.
If I'm unable too, let it become the death of me.
Life is bigger than me, it was already written.
Trying to figure out situations & how did I get in.
It's all purpose it's not a mistake, it's God's plan.
According on how you endure the situation, is what make you a man.
Live, learn, educate & inspire the youth.

Try to go beyond the sky, don't just stop at the roof.

Set your goals high, because Impossibility's are endless.

In this modern day, you keep it real with everyone, & still end up friendless.

You can't let nobody flaw, pull you down to their level.

Don't get contempt with one way, always have several.

Stay prayed up, keep your positive vibrations high.

Making this world a better place, be one of the reasons why.

Time Reveal.

It's hard to tell if people are for you, or really against you.
They act like they are down, they act sincere, but peep the actions they do.
They give you little inspiration no good news, but when it's bad they have a whole lot to say.
They really just a waste of time, spectators that's really in the way.
When God show up & show out, they act like it was in they favor, when they were wishing the worse.
Similar to when they show no emotion when you were alive, but so emotional when you in a hearse.
Most times I just want to be alone, I don't want no dealings.
Far away from fake people & they fake feelings.

Satan stay on his job, using people to deceive.

I believe none of what I hear, & half of what I perceive.

I keep positive vibes, & try my best to avoid negative frequencies.

My objective is to prosper, grow, & avoid any delinquencies.

Life hard & it isn't fair, as long as you got God, you are good anywhere.

As long as you face reality, accept the truth & never dare.

The Most High will make a way to see you through, to achieve your calling.

Time is of the Essence, never procrastinate or waste it stalling.

Proud Black American.

It's so hard to be a proud black American.
When oppressing, Imprisoning, & killing us seems to be U.S, Plans.
They separate us from our greats, but the bad identify with the whole race.
Then they call you racist like Malcolm X, when you throw the truth in they face.
They know you can still buy niggas, so they turn us against us.
The Willie Lynch syndrome is still in full effect, so you don't know who you can trust.
You can enlist into the armed forces fight for this country & still be look at as the enemy.
The police protect & serve the white

people, but they are the slave patrol, in the black community.

We get charged the same taxation.

But our rights we have no representation.

They hate us so much, but they want buy some land and send us back to Africa or give us or own state.

Or pay the reparations they owe, and let us decide our own fate.

And until this day you still have jigga'boos that love massa so much.

They so brainwashed with they own people; they are out of touch.

They don't know their true ancestor's past, just the white man history.

And don't believe nothing they own people teach them; they only believe his story.

They can send robots to mars, but don't know that black lives matter.

They started a controversy at first,
now they taking knees & holding
hands, do they sincerity even
Matter.
Knowing the history & the current
state of this country, it's hard to be a
proud black American.
We had a Mulato president telling us
to hope & yes, we can.
Black People get killed by whites &
the police that get charged but not
convicted.
Just being black alone make you a
suspect to get killed, charged, and
convicted.
We turned the other cheek, and it did
us no good.
When we start standing for what we
believe in, we can get understood.

Melancholy.

When you give someone all your heart and it get stepped on.
That feeling of hurt go far and beyond.
Even though I Am love, I descend from the Most High.
I can show it but not express it, the reason I don't know why.
As much as my heart been stabbed, cross, & broken, I'm surprise it still works.
With all the hate I been given, you'd think I'd be a miserable jerk.
My vibrations are too high & positive, my frequencies are equivalent.
My spirit is unbreakable, I am heaven sent.

Being in the flesh at time, I feel hurt
& pain.

Staying in touch with God keep me
focus & sane.
They only love you when you dead, &
I don't plan on dying no time soon.
Both of our hearts beat, but they
playing different tunes.
I put my heart and soul in these
words in my poems.
No fantasy or fiction, If I speak it's
an axiom.
I relax & meditate when I feel
melancholy.
Real recognize real likewise, you
ought to get to know me.

Trying To Understand Life

Seeking answers for purposes in life,

have me slowly losing my mind,
Finding conclusions, transitions my thoughts to be realign.
Life's enigmas after contemplating, remains unconfined.
Spiritual and soulless being beings, defines mankind
Questions are dedicatedly haunted, and never cease,
Only thing can stop me from pursuing, is being deceased.
Sanity unnoticeably crumbles, mentally seeking peace.
The crazy you seem to become, when your knowledge increase.
In pursuit of truths not understood,
Our cease for existences, to make life all good.
And share the knowledge, not have it confined under a hood.
And understand life, acknowledge the

things we misunderstood.
Thinking life's supposed to be like a movie directed by Scorsese.
Understanding's being grasp, but fleeting, now hazy,
The vibes aren't aligned with my soul, I can't become contempt, or lazy.
It seems trying to understand life, is driving me crazy

Destine.

I'm at a low of my life, but I know I'll rise like a Phoenix.
If I had them hating & in they feelings before, trust me they haven't seen nix.
That wasn't my intentions before, it want be my intentions now.
I'm living with the spirit of The All Most High, that's how I keep them

like wow.

I'm infused by the Sun, I'm melanated with a glow.

My third eye open & my chakras aligned I'm feeling like machismo.

Looking good because I was made in his image, I am who I am.

Positive vibes & positive frequencies, are how I connect with my fam.

I'll be transcending to the fifth dimension, when it's all said and done.

Leaving a legacy behind, for my daughter's & sons.

Praying I make my mother & sister proud, & all my love ones.

I'm all for the pro's, life is too short for the cons.

They can trap your body, but they can't trap your mind.

Life is about inspiring & prospering,
stay on your grind.
Fulfill your destiny, before your
journey end.
Or get stuck in this dimension, with
your soul in the wind.

Going Nowhere Fast

Running in circles, chasing empty
dreams,
Being stagnate, to the extreme.
Lost in a maze of endless schemes.
Pointless actions, with nothing to
redeem.
Gasping for air amidst the rushed
pace,
End up being the joke of, trying to be
the ace.
Going after nothing, on your fast

chase.

Going nowhere fast on your wild race.

Minutes pass, days blur, time slips away,

You're just a distraction, in the way.

Caught in this loop, like a moth in decay.

No plans for the future, just thinking about today.

Yearning for progress, yet standing steadfast,

Wasted time and energy, to end up last.

Plan and plot, so you can outlast.

In this world that moves quickly, going nowhere fast.

Phase IV Philosophical

Genocide

(White Supremacist + N!66@$)

From white supremacist plus the
system, & these n!66@$ & culture.
We are facing genocide, they feasting
on us like some vultures.
Being melanated you have to fear for
your life, getting pulled over for a
minor traffic violation.
Or being at the wrong urban function
at the wrong time, could be your life
expiration.
We are made in his image & of all the
elements of nature.

Is this why they hate us so much &
they hearts are as cold as glaciers.

Our own people have been mis-
influenced & miseducated for they
don't know no better.
A threat to nobody but your own
kind, you are born with common
sense you should know better.
White man we helped you civilized &
build this nation; we should be you all
best friends.
We got freed from slavery, now you
want all our lives to end.
Melanated people our ancestors are
rolling over in their graves.
The way most of us are looking,
doing, acting, & the way that we
behave.
Slavery ended, then came Jim Crow,
& now mass incarceration.

A war on drugs, when white people
are selling & doing more drugs than
anyone else in this nation.

We need to wake up & make changes
from what's going on.
Or continue to complain, protest, &
march singing songs.
You soulless beings your reign will
soon come to a demise.
Forever stuck in this 3rd dimension,
your soul can't surpass the heavenly
sky's.
To my melanated people, get your
positive vibrations, frequencies, &
energy back up, get in the tune
with nature.
And become the God's we were
meant to be, with the spirit all will
allure

Father's Day Away

Happy Father's Day, it's so hard
being away from my kids.
Reminiscing on time we were
together, & things that we did.
For mine, I'll do anything in this
world.
I can't wait until I have them back in
my world.
I keep them in my prays, every day &
night.
Asking The All Most High, to make
sure they are blessed & doing alright.
I'm a very proud father, I can leave
this Earth feeling accomplished.

& I still have a way to go, & so much
more to accomplished.

Two sons & three daughters, what
more could I ask for.
They are all what I need, I'm not
trying to have any more.
My first Father's Day being away, I'm
in so much pain.
I hear that there are always brighter
days after the rain.
I came so far, and got so much more
to go.
Started at seventeen, finished before
three zero.
I'm a very proud father, the feelings
I'm feeling is more than words can
say.
I'm so thankful of the love I receive,
on every Father's Day

IN TUNE WITH NATURE

I LOVE LOOKING IN THE SKY, FEELING &
SEEING THE SUN SHINE.
BEAMING ON MY THIRD EYE, TO ENLIGHTEN
MY MIND.
RECHARGE WITH POSITIVE ENERGY, TO LET
OFF GOOD VIBRATIONS.
I SPEAK WITH POSITIVE FREQUENCIES, SO I
COULD UPLIFT THIS NATION.
EVERYDAY ISN'T SUNNY, BUT I CAN STAND THE
RAIN.
WALKING AS IT PRECIPITATE, CONTEMPLATING
TO EASE MY PAIN.
NOTHING'S MORE RELAXING, THAN A WATER
FRONT.
NO MATTER LAKE, POND, RIVER, OR OCEAN,
REFLECTING ON LIFE, AND THINGS THAT I
WANT.
IT'S NOTHING LIKE TAKING SCROLLS ON THE
BEACH, EASING MY MIND.
ENJOYING THE FRESH AIR & SCENERY,
LEAVING ALL LIFE PROBLEMS BEHIND.
I ALSO LOVE TAKING SCROLLS ON A NATURE
TRAIL, TO SEEK SOME PEACE.
EVERY DAY IN THE CITY PROBLEMS SEEM TO
NEVER CEASE.
I LOVE BEING IN THE COUNTRY, WATCHING

THE STARS AT NIGHT.
TRYING TO STAY ALIGNED WITH THE STARS, TO
KEEP MY LIFE RIGHT.

NOTHING LIKE BEING IN THE HILLS OR
MOUNTAINS, WHERE THERE'S A WATERFALL.
LIFE IS LOVE, PEACE, & HAPPINESS, AND
NATURE PROVIDES IT ALL..

THE ALL NATURAL OVER WORLDY WAYS

WE CAN NEVER GET THEM TO RESPECT US,
UNTIL WE RESPECT OURSELF.
AND START HAVING LOYALTY, MORALS,
HONOR, LIFE ISN'T ALL ABOUT WEALTH.
THE MONETARY SYSTEM IS MAN MADE TO
KEEP YOU IN DEBT, IT WASN'T CREATED BY
GOD.
IT'S NOT EASY GOING AGAINST THE GRAIN,
BUT YOU GOT TO BE AGAINST ALL ODDS.
US AS A PEOPLE & THIS EARTH WILL BE HERE,
WHEN THE SYSTEM IS NO LONGER AROUND.
DEDICATING YOUR LIFE TO NOTHING,
CREATING A LEGACY THAT WILL NEVER BE
FOUND.
WE BEEN INTEGRATED A QUARTER OF THE
CENTURY, & MATTERS ARE STILL GETTING
WORSE.
INSTEAD OF UN-OPPRESSING US, THEY WANT
TO TELL US WE ARE CURSE.
PRAYING TO THE SAME GOD, WHY WANT ALL

THE SPIRITUAL PEOPLE UNITE.
BECAUSE DIVIDED WE FALL, THEY DON'T
WANT US TO STAND STRONG IN THE NAME OF
THE RIGHT.

STOP BEING INFLUENCED BY THE DEMONIC
MATTER THAT YOU HEAR & SEE.
PROTECT YOUR SPIRIT AT ALL COST, KEEP
POSITIVE, ENERGY, VIBES, & FREQUENCIES.

MY MELANATED PEOPLE, WE GOT TO GET IT
TOGETHER.

MY MELANATED BROTHERS & SISTERS WE MUST
UNITE & BUILD UP A NATION.
OR FOREVER BE SLAVES, BEING MISLED BY THE
OPPRESSOR EDUCATION.
WE KEEP DOING THE SAME THING, WE'LL KEEP
GETTING THE SAME RESULTS.
MAKING PHRASES COOL & APART OF OUR
CULTURE, THAT USE TO BE INSULTS.
IF YOU DON'T KNOW WHERE YOU COME FROM,
YOU WANT KNOW WHERE YOU ARE GOING.
WE ARE THE FOUNDER OF CIVILIZATION, GOD,
PROPHET, QUEEN, & KING.
WE ARE THE ORIGINATORS OF ART,
ENTERTAINMENT, LANGUAGE, &
PHILOSOPHIES.
THE DEVIL WANTS TO ERASE AND DISCREDIT
OUR PASS, SAYING WE STARTED AT SLAVERY.
SOLD & STOLE, AND BROUGHT TO THIS

COUNTRY, AND HELPED BUILT THIS NATION.
HOODWINKED, BAMBOOZLED, CONDITIONED,
& PROGRAMMED, SO WE WANT COME TO
REALIZATION.

TO KNOW IF WE DID IT FOR THEM, WE CAN DO
IT FOR OURSELVES.
WE CAN EDUCATE, GOVERN, & CREATE JOBS TO
ACCUMULATE OUR OWN WEALTH.
LIFE IS NOT ABOUT COMING FROM RAGS TO
RICHES, THEN BALL TO YOU FALL.
IT'S ABOUT GAINING MORE AND SETTING UP
THE NEXT GENERATION, SO THEY WANT
STALL.
WE ARE WARRIORS NOT THUGS AND SAVAGES,
THAT'S JUST A THREAT TO OUR OWN KIND.
AND START DYING & KILLING FOR REAL
CAUSES, STOP BEING FOLLOWERS USE OUR
OWN MIND.
KNOWING UNITED WE STAND & DIVIDED WE
FALL.
WE GOT TO GET IT TOGETHER, IN THE NAME
OF THE MOST HIGH OF ALL

THEY LOVE YOU, TO HATE YOU, TO LOVE YOU
AGAIN

THERE IS A THIN LINE BETWEEN LOVE AND
HATE.
I REFUSE TO LET ANYBODY MIX EMOTIONS
DETOUR MY FATE.

THE WORLD REVOLVES AROUND EVERYBODY,
EVERYONE WANTS THEIR WAY.
THEY LOVE YOU WHEN YOU UP, BUT WHEN
YOU ARE DOWN, THEY DON'T STAY.

LIFE IS TOO SHORT FOR GAMES; I HAVE NO
TIME TO PLAY.
FOR SELFISH MOTIVES AND SPITEFUL ACTIONS,
PEOPLE ARE QUICK TO BETRAY.
WHEN YOU AREN'T GIVING THEM NOTHING OR
THEY NOT BENEFITING FROM YOU.
THEY HATE YOU NOW, PLUS EVERYTHING YOU
DO.
FORGETTING ALL THE LOVE AND THE GOOD
THINGS YOU DID.
OFF THE FACE OF THIS EARTH, YOU THEY WISH
THEY CAN GET RID.
NOW THE PENDULUM SWING, AND THINGS ARE
BACK GREAT.
NOW THEY LOVE YOU AGAIN AS IF THEY
NEVER HATE.
SOME PEOPLE ARE PROPS IN OUR LIFE, OR JUST
THERE FOR A SEASON.
DIVIDE THE LIGHT FROM THE DARKNESS,
THOUGHT OFFSPRING REASON.
IF I LOVE YOU, I LOVE YOU FOR LIFE, THROUGH
THE UPS AND DOWNS.
I'LL UPLIFT, ENLIGHTEN, & BRING YOU JOY,
TURN A SMILE FROM YOUR FROWN.
I FUNCTION OFF POSITIVE VIBES, I HAVE NO
PATIENCE FOR NEGATIVE PEOPLE.
IF I LOVE YOU IN THE FIRST PART, I'LL LOVE
YOU IN THE SEQUEL.

LIKE THE SUN (LIGHT & HEAT)

THEY KNOW THAT I'LL RISE LIKE THE
PHOENIX, & SHINE LIKE THE SUN.
REFUSE TO SETTLE FOR LESS, AIM TO BE
NUMBER ONE.
ENDURING MINOR SETBACKS FOR MAJOR COME
BACKS.
ELIMINATING NEGATIVE PEOPLE, SO I CAN
NEVER GET THROWN OFF TRACK.
TIME IS THE ESSENCE, THE MOST PRECIOUS
THING IN THIS WORLD.
NEXT COME YOUR MOM, YOUR KIDS, FAMILY, &
YOUR GIRL.
BUILDING A FOUNDATION, FULFILLING, YOUR
DESTINY.
PRAISING THE MOST HIGH, BEING THE BEST
PERSON, YOU CAN BE.
NEVER SELL YOUR SOUL, CONFIRMING TO THE
WORLDLY WAYS.
CONTEMPLATE TO MAKE HISTORY, INSTEAD OF
MAKING PLAYS.
KEEP FOLLOWING THE SAME ACTIONS,
GETTING THE SAME CONSEQUENCES.
ENDING UP IN THE GRAVEYARDS, BEHIND
WALLS, & BARBWIRE FENCES.
IT'S THE SAME OL 'STORY AND THE SAME OL
'BROTHER STUCK.

WE TOO BUSY TRY N TO TURN UP OR CHASING
AFTER BUCKS.
A MILL WALKING, WITH DREAMS TO FLIP A KEY.

MADE IT LEGITIMATELY BUT GLAMORIZE
CRIMINALITY.
WE STILL STAGNATE OR REGRESSING.
JUST A BUNCH OF USE TO BE STORIES, NO
PROGRESSING.
NEVER MEDITATE, REVALUATE, STEADY STILL
STRESSING.
FAITH WITHOUT WORK IS DEAD, BUT PRAYING
FOR A BLESSING.
KEEP GOING THRU THE SAME DRAMA, NEVER
LEARN A LESSON.
THEN THEY GET IN THEIR FEELINGS, AND
START CONFESSING.
IT'S ALL LOVE, POSITIVE VIBES.
WHEN YOU REALLY REAL, YOU HAVE NOTHING
TO HIDE.
IF THEY DON'T HAVE A STORY, THEY'LL MAKE
UP ONE.
I'M SO ENLIGHTEN, THEY REVOLVE AROUND
ME, LIKE THE SUN.

THE ALL PLAN

I CAME TO FAR TO BE DROPPED OFF HERE.
I'M NOT PERFECT, BUT I'M SINCERE.
FROM BEING AT THE BEST OF MY BEST.
NOW I HAVE TO SETTLE FOR LESS.
I LEARN TO HAVE FAITH, AND LET GO OF THE

STRESS.
PRAYING TO THE ALL, TO REMAIN TO BE BLESS.
I KNOW IT WAS WRITTEN, IT'S BEYOND MY
CONTROL.

I TAKE IT IN STRIDE, I GOT TO KEEP A HOLD.
WE FALL DOWN BUT WE GET UP.
I REMAIN THE SAME, WHEN IT WAS EMPTY, TO
WHEN IT FILLETH MY CUP.
I'M SO FOCUSED, BUT CAN'T SEE WHAT THE
FUTURE BEHOLDS.
IT'S ALL THE ALL'S PLAN, THIS IS WHAT I WAS
TOLD.
POSITIVE ENERGY, FREQUENCIES, AND
VIBRATIONS, SO I CAN TRANSCEND.
NO NEGATIVE ENERGY, FREQUENCIES, OR
VIBRATIONS, SO I WANT SIN.
I STAY PRAYED UP, SO I CAN BE THE BEST THAT
I CAN BE.
I'M TRYING TO TAKE THIS LIFE BEYOND, AS FAR
AS I CAN SEE.
NOTHING'S IMPOSSIBLE I KNOW I CAN.
ACHIEVE & OBTAIN IT'S THE ALL PLAN.

TAKE ADVANTAGE OF A GOOD HEART

HAVING A GOOD HEART, ALWAYS GET YOU
HURT IN THE END.
NO MATTER WHO YOU DEALING WITH FAMILY,
LOVERS, & FRIENDS.
THEY LOVE YOU WHEN YOU GOT IT, DON'T
KNOW IF YOU DON'T.
THEY ASK YOU TO DO THINGS, IF YOU ASKED

THEM, THEY KNOW THEY WANT.
NOT KNOWING AS MUCH LOVE YOU GOT TO
GIVE, IT CAN TURN TO HATE.

UNLESS YOU ARE IN TUNE TO STAY ON A
HIGHER REALM, POSITIVE VIBRATE.
SOME PEOPLE THINK THEY HAVE ALL THE
SENSE, UNTIL THEY HAVE NONE.
IN NEED OF A PLAY STATION OR XBOX,
BECAUSE I'M NOT THE ONE.
NO GOOD DEEDS GO UNPUNISHED AT ALL.
THE ALL MOST HIGH IS THE ONLY RELIABLE
SOURCE YOU CAN CALL.
YOU'LL BE DAMN IF YOU DO, DAMN IF YOU
DON'T.
IT'S ALRIGHT TO SHOW TOUGH LOVE, THE
TIMES THAT YOU WANT.
SOME PEOPLE ARE HEARTLESS, LOVERS OF
THEM SELF.
NO MATTER HOW HARD YOU TRY TO STAY IN
THE RIGHT, THEY ALWAYS ON THE LEFT.
ALWAYS STAY REAL TO THE END FROM THE
START.
BAD PEOPLE TAKE ADVANTAGE OF A GOOD
HEART.
FEEBLE MINDED PEOPLE TAKE KINDNESS FOR
WEAKNESS.
BE UNBELIEVERS, UNTIL YOU SHOW THEM
YOUR UNIQUENESS.
MY HEART BEEN FATALLY WOUNDED SEVERAL
TIMES, BUT STILL FIND A WAY TO OPERATE.
IT ONLY MADE MY HEART STRONGER, NOW IT'S
TEFLON TOWARDS ABUSE AND THE HATE.

RESPECT THE QUEEN

MUCH RESPECT AND POWER TO MY
MELANATED QUEENS.
THE LOVE FROM YOU IS NECESSARY BY ANY
MEANS.
US WARRIORS NEED TO GET OUR QUEENS BACK
TO THE THRONE.
SO, LOVE, PEACE, AND HAPPINESS CAN BE
RESTORED TO THIS EARTH, WHERE IT
BELONGS.
THROUGHOUT TIME THEY BEEN
DISRESPECTED, NOW SOME DON'T RESPECT
THEMSELVES.
NO LONGER SEEKING TRUE LOVE, IT'S ABOUT
FAME & WEALTH.
THE FIRST BEING IN THIS WORLD, NO ONE
CAME BEFORE YOU.
GOD CHOSEN PEOPLE OR MAYBE GOD IS YOU.
THROUGHOUT ANY STRUGGLE, YOU ALWAYS
KEEP YOUR HEAD UP.
IT'S NOTHING WE CAN DO, WHEN A WOMAN'S
FED UP.
THE MOST BEAUTIFUL FEMALE IN THIS WORLD.
YOU ARE MY SOUL SISTERS, MELANATED GIRLS.
ENVY NO ONE, THEY ALL WANT TO BE LIKE
YOU.
FROM EVERYTHING, FROM WHAT YOU WEAR,
SAY, OR DO.
THE ALL MOST HIGH CREATED SUCH A
PERFECT BEING.
MELANATED BROTHERS WE NEED TO GET IT
TOGETHER, AND RESPECT OUR QUEEN.

AS ABOVE, SO BELOW

MOST PEOPLE WANT TO GO HEAVEN, LIVING
WITH LOW MORALS.
BE A BURDEN ALL YOUR LIFE, WHEN YOU
DIE,THEY GIVE YOU YOUR FLORALS.
IF THERE'S A HELL BELOW, WE ALL GOING TO
GO.
FOR THINGS THAT WE ARE AWARE OF, AND
SOME WE DON'T KNOW.
FROM A SYSTEM WE ARE BORN INTO, TO
SURVIVE WE MUST GO WITH THE FLOW.
THEY SAY YOU ONLY LIVE ONCE, SO LIFE WE
AREN'T TRYING TO BLOW.
BUT ENERGY NEVER DIES, I'M VIBING HIGH,
TRANSCENDING TO THE COSMOS.
ON TO THE 5TH DIMENSION, NOT ON THE 3RD
STUCK AS A GHOST.
IT STARTS AS A THOUGHT, TO BECOME
REALITY.
IF WE WEREN'T MISGUIDED OR MISEDUCATED,
THE THINGS IN LIFE, WE CAN DO OR WE
CAN BE.
A LOT PEOPLE HAVE NEGATIVE SPIRITS &
ENERGY, OR LOW VIBRATIONS & FREQUENCIES.
I'M IN TUNE WITH THE ALL, I DON'T WANT
NONE OF THAT AROUND ME.
YOUR REALITY IS ALL IN YOUR MIND.
THINK POSITIVE & POSITIVE RESULTS WANT BE
HARD TO FIND.
SEEK KNOWLEDGE, THERE ARE THINGS YOU
NEED TO KNOW.
AS BELOW, SO ABOVE, AS ABOVE, SO BELOW.

BLACK LIVES ARE THE MATTER

(THE CREATORS OF CIVILIZATION)

INSPIRED BY J.A, ROGERS

A NEGRO ASTRONOMER NAME BENJAMIN
BANNEKER MADE THE FIRST CLOCK IN
AMERICA IN 1754.
STAY WOKE GET YOUR COFFEE, ORIGINATING
FROM CAFFA ETHIOPIA, WHERE IT WAS FIRST
USED & STILL WILDLY GROW.
THE OLDEST DRAWING AND CRAVINGS WERE
THOSE OF A NEGRO 15,000 YEARS AGO.
IN SOUTH AMERICA, INDIA, PALESTINE,
NORTHEN SPAIN, & SOUTHERN FRANCE
ANYWHERE IN THE WORLD YOU GO.
THE OLDEST REPRESENTATION OF THE HUMAN
BODY IS A STATUE OF A MELANATED WOMAN
CALLED VENUS OF WILLENDORF.
MELANATED WOMAN IS DEITY, PRICELESS IS
HER WORTH.
THE BLACK SPANIARD AKA BEETHOVEN IS THE
WORLD'S GREATEST MUSICIAN.
AND HIS TEACHER THE IMMORTAL JOSEPH
HAYDN ANOTHER NEGRO GREAT MUSICIAN.
THE GRIMALDI, A MELANATED RACE LIVED IN
EUROPE 12,000 YEARS AGO.
THE THINGS THEY SHOULD TEACH US IN
SCHOOL BUT DON'T WANT US TO KNOW.
THE GREAT PYRAMID, ONE OF THE SEVEN
WONDERS OF THE ANCIENT WORLD, WAS BUILT
BY A NEGRO NAME CHEOPS.

COVERS 13 ACRES, 451 FEET HIGH, BUILT BY
100,000 MEN WITH 2,500,000 BLOCKS.
ANCIENT EGYPT HAD AT LEAST 18 ETHIOPIAN
OR UNMIXED NEGRO RULERS, THE BEST
KNOWN IS PIANKHI.
WE WERE CREATED IN HIS IMAGE, THE CLOSET
TO THE ALL IN THE SKY.
THE EMPEROR HAILE SELASSIE I, ETHIOPIA
RULER HIS ANCESTRY TRACES TO KING
SOLOMON & THE QUEEN OF SHEBA, &
BEYOND CUSH, 6280 B.C.
BEFORE COLUMBUS, NEGROES LIVED IN
AMERICA THOUSANDS OF YEARS, PROOF IS
CRAVINGS OF US AS GODS, WHO WE
TRULY BE.

BLACK LIVES ARE THE MATTER: PART 2

(THE CREATORS OF CIVILIZATION)

INSPIRED BY J.A, ROGERS

THE ORIGIN OF SLAVE WAS SLAV WHITE
PEOPLE, RUSSIANS CAPTURED BY GERMANS.
THE FIRST SLAVES IN THE UNITED STATES
WERE NOT BLACK BUT WHITE EUROPEANS.
DIED LIKE FLIES ON THE SLAVES' SHIPS
COMING ACROSS.
OUT OF 1,500, 1,100 OVERBOARD THEY HAD TO
TOSS.
JAN ERNEST MATZELIGER INVENTED THE
FIRST MACHINE FOR SEWING SOLES OF SHOES

TO THE UPPERS.
REVOLUTIONIZED THE INDUSTRY AND GAVE
SHOES SUPREMACY IN THE UNITED STATES THE
UPPERS.
MOSES IN THE BIBLE, WAS A BLACK MAN.
WHEN GOD TOLD MOSES TO PUT HIS HAND
INTO HIS BOSOM, IT TURNS WHITE, A MIRACLE
THEN TURNED BLACK AGAIN.
ALL CHARACTERS IN THE BIBLE ARE MOSTLY
MELANATED.
THE TRUTH HURT, THEN IT SET YOU FREE, IF
YOU HATE IT.
THE REAL FATHER OF MEDICINE WAS ANCIENT
EGYPTIAN IMHOTEP.
IF THEY TEACH US OUR REAL HISTORY IN
CLASS, WE'D PROBABLY NEVER WOULD HAVE
SLEPT.
DR. DANIEL WILLIAMS A CHICAGO SURGEON
WAS THE FIRST TO PERFORM A SUCCESSFUL
OPERATION ON THE HUMAN HEART.
THEY LIE ABOUT OUR CONTRIBUTIONS TO THE
WORLD; THESE DEVILS DON'T HAVE NO HEART.
NEARLY ALL THE ANCIENT GODS OF THE NEW
& OLD WORLD WERE BLACK AND HAD WOOLLY
HAIR.
THE DEVIL IS DECEIVING GOT US LIVING A LIE,
THAT'S WHY LIFE ISN'T FAIR.

DAILY PRAYER

FROM WHEN I WAKE UP TO WHEN I GO TO BED,
AND SEVERAL TIMES BETWEEN I PRAY.
I THANK THE ALL MOST HIGH FOR LETTING ME
SEE ANOTHER DAY.
I PRAY FOR A PRODUCTIVE BLESS DAY, AND TO
KEEP THE DEVIL OUT MY WAY.
I PRAY TO BE ENLIGHTENED BY THE SUN, AND
FEEL THE SUN'S RAY.
I THANK THE ALL FOR MY WISDOM,
KNOWLEDGE, AND INTELLIGENCE.
I THANK THE ALL FOR BEING BLESS, WITH MY
SEVEN SENSES.
I THANK THE ALL MOST HIGH FOR BLESSING
ME WITH KIDS.
I PRAY FOR FORGIVENESS FOR ALL THE WRONG
THAT I DID.
I THANK THE ALL FOR BLESSING ME WITH MY
MOMMA.
I PRAY THE ALL KEEP ME AWAY FROM HARM &
DRAMA.
I THANK THE ALL MOST HIGH FOR BLESSING
ME WITH MY SIS.
I PRAY FOR ALL MY FAMILY DAILY, WHEN I'M
AWAY THEY ARE SURELY MISS.
I THANK THE ALL MOST HIGH FOR BLESSING
ME WITH MY DAD.
I PRAY TO MY QUEEN, THAT I'M THE BEST SHE
EVER HAD.
I PRAY NOT TO GO TO PRISON, NOT TO GO TO
JAIL.

I PRAY TO KEEP ME AWAY FROM SIN, NOT TO
GO TO HELL.
I PRAY THAT THE I FULFILL MY DESTINY ON
THIS EARTH.
I THANK THE ALL MOST HIGH FOR MAKING ME
WHAT I'M WORTH.
I PRAY TO HAVE A PROSPEROUS DAY, WITH NO
SIN.
I THANK THE ALL MOST HIGH FOR
EVERYTHING AMEN.

725 UNTIL…

ONCE UPON A TIME, THERE WAS A BIRTH OF A
BEAUTIFUL MELANATED BOY.
BORN TO A GREAT FAMILY, HIS MOTHER PRIDE
AND JOY.
VERY INTELLIGENT, READY TO TAKE ON THE
WORLD.
HE HAD A SISTER OLDER THAN HIM, HIS
MOTHER ONLY GIRL.
FROM A YOUNG AGE, HE WAS DESTINING TO
BE.
EVERYTHING WAS ON TRACK, UNTIL THE AGE
OF ONE THREE.
HE HAD TO GROW UP FAST, SO HE CAN TAKE
CARE OF HIMSELF.
STARTED DOING WRONG, EVEN THOUGH HE
KNOWS THAT WASN'T HIMSELF.
LIFE ISN'T FAIR, IT'S ALL ABOUT SURVIVAL &
LIVING GOOD.
BY ANY MEANS NECESSARY DO ANYTHING YOU
COULD.

BAD INFLUENCES, IF WE KNEW BETTER, WE'D
DO BETTER.
EVERY CRUSH HE HAD, NEVER STOPPED UNTIL
HE GETS HER.
GOT BACK ON TRACK, GRADUATED HAD A SON.
CHANGED HIS LIFE AROUND, WOKE HIM UP
LIKE THE SUN.
THEN CAME NUMBER TWO, & THREE
DAUGHTERS AFTER THAT.
ALWAYS BEEN A GREAT FATHER, TO HIM YOU
HAVE TO TILT YOUR HAT.
AT ONCE IT'S WAS SPORTS, BUT MUSIC BECAME
THE LOVE OF HIS LIFE.
HE HAD SEXUAL RELATIONSHIPS, ONCE CLOSE
BUT NEVER HAD A WIFE.
MANY TIMES, HE FELL DOWN, BUT GOT BACK
UP.
ALWAYS STOOD ON HIS OWN, NEVER HAD
BACK UP.
GOD GIVE HIS TOUGHEST BATTLES TO THE
STRONGEST PEOPLE.
HE COULD HAVE THE SAME SIMILARITIES WITH
SOMEONE & WANT BE EQUAL.
HE ALWAYS BEEN HIS OWN MAN.
& UNAPOLOGETICALLY AFRICAN.
IF IT COULD BE DONE, HE KNEW THAT HE CAN.
ALWAYS LOOK OUT FOR THE PEOPLE, NEVER
SELFISH FOR WEALTH.
BECAME VEGAN, NEVER PUT NOTHING BEFORE
HIS HEALTH.
IF IT'S A WILL IT'S A WAY, SURELY, HE'S
DETERMINED.

POSITIVE SPIRIT AND SOUL UNLIKELY TO
COMMIT SIN.
THE DEVIL STAYS BUSY BUT THE ALL MOST
HIGH BLESS.
AT FIRST THE TRUTH HURT, BUT HE GETS IT
OFF HIS CHEST.
THEN IT SET YOU FREE, SO YOU CAN BE YOUR
BEST.
SKY'S THE LIMIT, NEVER SETTLE FOR LESS.
IF BEING FAKE IS THE TREND, HE'LL BE
UNPOPULAR BEING TRILL.
UNTIL FOREVER AND A DAY, FROM 725 UNTIL.

METAMORPHOSE

I'M IN TRANSFORMATION, I'M LEARNING TO
TRUST THE PROCESS.
IT'S A HARD TRANSITION, I'M UNDER A LOT OF
DISTRESS.
SOMETIMES YOU ARE UP, SOMETIMES YOU ARE
DOWN, BUT REMEMBER LIFE GOES ON.
MONEY ISN'T REAL, IT'S ONLY THE MEMORIES
THAT REMEMBERED, WHEN YOUR DEAD AND
GONE.
YOU FIND OUT WHO WAS REALLY DOWN FOR
YOU, WHEN YOUR DOWN AND OUT.
AND THE ONES WHO GIVE FAKE LOVE, JUST TO
GET SOME CLOUT.
TIME IS OF THE ESSENCE, AND I HAVE NONE
TO WASTE.
SOME PEOPLE HAVE NO PROBLEM TELLING
LIES, LOOKING YOU RIGHT IN THE FACE.

THANK GOD THERE'S A GOD, BECAUSE IF WE
DEPENDED ON MAN, WE'D BE DOOMED.
THE VIOLENCE, DEATH, & DESTRUCTION
WOULD NEVER STOP, IT'LL ALWAYS RESUME.
NO MATTER WHO AND WHAT THEIR
RELATIONSHIP TO YOU IN LIFE, SOME PEOPLE
IS JUST NO GOOD.
THEY'LL NEVER OVERSTAND, AND THAT'S
UNDER STOOD.
IF THEY ARE NO GOOD RIGHT HERE, THEY'LL
BE NO GOOD WHERE YOU ARE TRYING TO GO.
I'M ON A HIGH POSITIVE WAVE, MOVING
FORWARD IS MY FLOW.
NOTHING GROWS BEING COMFORTABLE, YOU
GOT TO EXPERIENCE SOME PAIN.
CONVERT FOR THE BETTER, DON'T LIVE LIFE
IN VAIN.

REDEEM

I'M TRYING TO REDEEM THE TIME THAT I LOST.
WHAT I REDEEMED, PRICELESS IS THE COST.
I THOUGHT I LOST IT ALL, BUT THE ALL MADE
ME GREATER.
MY VIBRATIONS & FREQUENCIES SO HIGH, I
CAN'T SEE OR HEAR A HATER.
ON TO THE NEXT, BEING THE BEST THAT I CAN
BE.
POSITIVE ENERGY AND LOVE ARE ALL I'M
TRYING TO FEEL AND SEE.

ENJOYING EVERY MINUTE IN LIFE, BECAUSE
YOU CAN'T GET IT BACK WHEN IT'S OVER.
IN THE SAME STATE OF MIND, YOU CAN'T
CONTINUE TO HOVER.
I METAMORPHOSIS, TO A HIGHER BEING.
BELIEVE NONE OF WHAT YOU HEAR, HALF OF
WHAT YOU ARE SEEING.
INSTEAD OF DWELLING ON, LEARN TO SOLVE
THE PROBLEMS YOU ARE FLEEING.
THIS WORLD IS A LOCK, YOU GOT TO BECOME
THE KEY IN.
IT'S AN AMAZING FEELING WHEN YOU CAN
SMILE AT YOURSELF IN THE MIRROR, & SLEEP
PEACEFUL AT NIGHT.
ALWAYS BE THE BIGGER PERSON, TWO
WRONGS DON'T MAKE A RIGHT.
LIFE CAN ALWAYS BE BETTER, THAN WHAT IT
SEEMS.
IF YOU THINK IT, YOU CAN ACHIEVE IT, IF YOU
DEEM.

DEARLY DEPARTED…

EVEN THOUGH YOU ARE GONE, YOU ARE
NEVER FORGOTTEN.
IT'S HARD TO DISTINGUISH, SINCE NO LONGER
MY LIFE YOU ARE NOT IN.
I'LL MOURN YOU TILL I JOIN YOU, YOU'LL
ALWAYS BE APART OF ME.
I THANK THE ALL MOST HIGH FOR THE TIMES
TOGETHER, WE GOT TO BE.

LONG LIVE YOUR LEGACY, THROUGH ME
YOU'LL LIVE ON.
YOU ARE TRULY LOVED & MISSED, FROM
EVERYONE THAT YOU TRULY KNOWN.
IT'S SO HARD TO SAY GOODBYE TO
YESTERDAY, BUT TOMORROW GONNA COME.
IT'S BEEN A LONG JOURNEY TO WHERE WE ARE
AT NOW, TO WHERE WE CAME FROM.
THE ALL MOST HIGH DON'T MAKE MISTAKES,
IT'S ALL GOD'S PLAN.
WE ARE GONNA CELEBRATE YOUR LIFE, UNTIL
WE MEET AGAIN.
YOU'LL ALWAYS BE IN MY PRAYERS, I'M
THANKFUL FOR YOU FOR BEING IN MY
LIFETIME.
I NEVER IMAGINE THIS DAY WILL COME, WHEN
YOU AREN'T PHYSICALLY ON MY LIFELINE.
ONE DAY YOU ARE HERE, THE NEXT DAY YOU
ARE GONE.
DEPARTED TO THE HEAVENLY SKIES, TO SIT
ON YOUR THRONE.
THE MEMORIES WE HAD WILL NEVER PASS
OVER, MY LOVE WILL NEVER CEASE.
UNTIL WE MEET AGAIN BLESS YOUR SOUL,
ETERNALLY REST IN PEACE.

REST IN PEACE TO SHON SHON, PHYLLIS
CANADY, & CLAYTON BROWN

#CIBLE #CUEINTUTIONBEFORELEAVINGEARTH
#DEARLYDEPARTED #RESTINPEACE

THE DEVIL STAYS BUSY

IN THIS CRAZY WORLD, THE DEVIL STAYS BUSY.
SATAN CAN'T LOWER MY VIBES OR KNOCK ME
OFF MY GRIZZY.
THE DEVIL WILL USE ANYONE HE CAN TO TRY
TO GET AT YOU.
MOSTLY WEAK SPIRITS AND SOULLESS BEINGS
IS WHO SATAN WORK THROUGH.
HE HATES TO SEE WHEN YOUR SOUL IS
ENLIGHTENED, AND YOUR SPIRIT IS HIGH.
PLUS, WHEN YOUR ENERGY SO CHARGED, YOU
CAN BELIEVE YOU CAN FLY.
THE MASTER OF DECEPTION, MOST OF THE
WORLD HAS BEEN DECEIVED.
THE HATE GROWS STRONGER & STRONGER,
AFTER EVERY BLESSING YOU RECEIVE.
SO WICKED, HE'D WANT TO KILL YOU AFTER
YOU SAVE HIS LIFE.
EVERYTHING COULD BE ALL GOOD, AND THEY
STILL ACT TRIFE.
THE DEVIL MUST DO EVIL, BECAUSE LOVE AND
JOY CAUSE HIM PAIN.
YOU MALICIOUS PEOPLES AN ABOMINATION,
HATE IS IN THE BLOOD OF YOUR VEINS.
LIVING IN SIN, DO EVERYTHING OUT OF SPITE.
THEY POWER UP OFF DOING WRONG, SO THEY
DON'T WANT TO BE RIGHT.
SATAN WANT TO CORRUPT ME WITH HIS
DEMONIC SPIRIT, BUT MY AURA HIGH.
DOING EVERYTHING IN HIS STRENGTH TO
MAKE ME MISERABLE, HOPING I DIE.

I WAS CREATED IN HIS IMAGINE, I HAVE THE
SPIRIT & SOUL OF THE ALL MOST HIGH.
I'M TOO RIGHTEOUS TO GO TO HELL, I'M GONE
LIVE IN THE SKY.

FAMILY OVER EVERYTHING

FAMILY OVER EVERYTHING, THERE'S NOTHING
I'LL PUT BEFORE MINE.
I THANK THE ALL MOST HIGH DAILY, FOR
BLESSING ME WITH MINE.
THE REASON WHY I'M LIVING, THE REASON
WHY I GRIND.
IF WE AREN'T ALL BLINGING, THEN I DON'T
WANT TO SHINE.
WE AREN'T ALL PERFECT, WE ALL HAVE UPS &
DOWN.
THROUGH THE THICK & THIN, FAMILY WILL
ALWAYS BE AROUND.
THAT'S HOW WE LEARN TO GROW, AND MAKE
OUR BOND STRONG.
IT'S NOTHING LIKE MEETING UP COMING
TOGETHER, WHERE ALL OF US BELONG.
IF ANY OF MY LOVE ONES CALL ME, I'LL
ALWAYS BE THERE.
SOME OF US IS MISFORTUNE, LIFE ISN'T ALWAYS
FAIR.
AS LONG AS WE STICK TOGETHER, AND SHOW
TENDER LOVE AND CARE.
AND KEEP THE LOVE SO STRONG, YOU CAN
FEEL IT IN THE AIR.

I'LL DIE ABOUT MY BLOOD, AND EVEN DO LIFE
IN PRISON.
I'D DEDICATE MY LIFE IF THEY ARE DOWN, TO
HELP THEM RISEN.
THESE ARE NATURAL INSTINCTS FROM GOD TO
BE.
PUT NOTHING IN LIFE OVER YOUR FAMILY.

BIRTHDAY AWAY

7-25-21

IT'S HARD CELEBRATING A BIRTHDAY AWAY
FROM FAMILY AND FRIENDS.
BEING AWAY IN A TERRIBLE SITUATION,
WAITING FOR IT TO END.
CALLED AND TALKED TO MY MOTHER, IT
BROUGHT TEARS TO MY EYES.
LOOKING AT THE WINDOW THINKING ABOUT
HER, LOOKING AT THE BEAUTIFUL SKIES.
I TALKED TO MY BIG SIS, SHE BRIGHTEN UP MY
DAY.
SHE LET ME KNOW EVERYTHING GOING TO BE
ALRIGHT, ON MY BIRTHDAY AWAY.
I STAYED PRAYED UP, TO STAY FOCUS &
MAINTAIN.
TO KEEP MY SPIRIT HIGH, AND TO KEEP ME
SANE.
WAITING UNTIL I'M ABLE TO SPEAK TO MY
KIDS.

REMINISCING ON LAST YEAR HOW GOOD
THINGS WERE, & THE THINGS THAT
I DID.
I THANK 'THE ALL MOST HIGH, FOR LETTING
ME SEE ANOTHER YEAR.
AND GIVING ME THE POWER, STRENGTH,
COURAGE, PLUS NO FEAR.
I KNOW GOD DIDN'T BRING ME THIS FAR, TO
DROP ME OFF HERE.
BEING RIGHTEOUS AND ENLIGHTEN PLUS
SINCERE.
I'M BLESSED TO CELEBRATE ANOTHER YEAR
ON THIS EARTH.
EVEN THOUGH IT'S A LONELY ONE, I'M
THANKFUL FOR THIS DAY OF MY BIRTH.

PHASE V

DETERMINATION

INSPIRATION

ANYTHING YOU PUT YOUR MIND TOO, BEST
BELIEVE YOU CAN DO IT.
IF THERE'S A WILL, THERE'S AWAY, HAVE FAITH
AND YOU CAN GET THROUGH IT.
ALL YOU GOT TO DO IS PUSH, MEANING PRAY

UNTIL SOMETHING HAPPENS.
KEEP IT REAL WITH YOURSELF AND OTHERS, IT
TAKES LESS ENERGY THAN CAPPING.
THE ALL MOST HIGH, DON'T MAKE NO
MISTAKES.
SOMETHINGS ARE BEYOND OUR
UNDERSTANDING; IT TAKES LONGER TO
INTAKE.
YOU DON'T BECOME A GOOD SAILOR, IN STILL
WATERS.
ALWAYS HAVE FAITH, IN THE HEAVENLY
FATHER.
JUST REMEMBER, PRESSURE CREATE
DIAMONDS.
ALWAYS GIVE IT YOUR ALL, UNTIL YOU DIE
MAN.
AIM TO BE THE BEST, NEVER SETTLE FOR LESS.
YOU'LL CONTINUE TO GO THROUGH THE SAME
TRIALS, UNTIL YOU PASS THE TEST.
BE QUICK TO LISTEN, AND SLOW TO TALK.
BEING RIGHTEOUSNESS IS THE BEST PATH TO
WALK.
HAVE A PURE HEART, DO GOOD DEEDS WITH
NO HESITATION.
PRAY TO THE ALL MOST HIGH, WHEN YOU
NEED SOME INSPIRATION.

TOO SMART FOR THEY OWN GOOD

SOME PEOPLE COULD BE IN GOD PRESENTS,
AND STILL WANT DO RIGHT.
KNOW THEY DEAD WRONG, AND STILL WANT
TO FIGHT.

WILL TELL YOU A LIE, WHILE LOOKING RIGHT
IN THE EYE.
STAY IN SOME DRAMA, AND ACT IF AS THEY
DON'T KNOW WHY.
WILL DO ANYTHING TO MAKE YOU LOOK BAD,
TO VALIDATE THEY WRONG DOING.
YOU SUPPORT THEM, IN RETURN FOR YOU
THEY ON THE SIDELINE BOOING.
ALWAYS WANT SOMETHING, BUT NEVER HAVE
NOTHING TO GIVE.
JUST ANOTHER LOST SOUL, FROM THE LIFE
THAT THEY LIVE.
WOULD ASK YOU TO DO A FAVOR, THAT THEY
WOULDN'T NEVER DO FOR YOU.
WHEN YOU CUT THEM OFF, THEY THINK YOU
ACTING FUNNY, AS IF THEY DON'T HAVE NO
CLUE.
THAT'S WHY I STAY TO MYSELF, BECAUSE I
DON'T WANT PEOPLE PUSHING THEY
PROBLEMS ON ME.
LIFE IS TOO SHORT, AND I'M TRYING TO LIVE
FOR ETERNITY.
I'M VIBING ON A HIGH PLANE NO TIME FOR
NEGATIVITY.
MOST PEOPLE CAUSE THEY OWN DEMISE, JUST
SIT BACK AND SEE.
YOU CAN'T TELL THEM NOTHING, BECAUSE
THEY HAVE ALL THE SENSE.
TOO SMART FOR THEY OWN GOOD, AND SWEAR
THAT YOU ARE DENSE.

TOMORROW NOT PROMISED

I'M NOT PERFECT, BUT I'M BLESSED ENOUGH
TO KNOW RIGHT FROM WRONG.
KEEP PREFORMING THE SAME ACTIONS, YOU'LL
BE SINGING THE SAME OLD SONGS.
YOU CAN'T ALWAYS POINT THE FINGER, YOU
GOT TO CHECK YOURSELF.
YOU MIGHT BE FOOLING YOU, BUT TO OTHERS
YOU ARE NOT SO STEALTH.
RESPECT IS GIVING, TO WHERE RESPECT IS DUE.
LIFE HAS MANY OPTIONS, IT'S NOT ALL ABOUT
YOU.
I LIVED BY THE MOTTO, LESS PEOPLE LESS
PROBLEMS.
I'M SURROUNDED BY ANGELS, & YOU ARE
POSSESSED BY A GOBLIN.
SOMETIMES YOU HAVE TO LEARN, TO AGREE
TO DISAGREE.
SOME PEOPLE FOLLOW RELIGION, SOME
FOLLOW SPIRITUALITY.
WHILE OTHERS ARE CONFORMED TO THE
WORLD, MISGUIDED LOST SOULS.
THESE ARE MY WORDS OF WISDOM; I'M
PUTTING IT ALL ON SCROLLS.
WE NEED TO GET BACK TO LOVING, BUILDING
EACH OTHER UP.
BEFORE IT'S ALL OVER, AND OUR TIME IS UP.
THEN THINK BACK AND SAY, WHAT WE COULD
OF, SHOULD OF, & WOULD, OF DONE.
WE ARE ALL THRIVING FOR THE LOVE, PEACE &
HAPPINESS, IF WE CAME TOGETHER, WE BEEN
COULD HAVE WON.

TOMORROW NOT PROMISED, SO LET'S GIVE
OUR ALL TODAY.
NEVER LET THE POSITIVE ENERGY STOP, PASS
IT LIKE A RELAY.

DECEPTION

EVERYTHING ISN'T ALWAYS WHAT IT SEEMS.
INSTEAD OF FOCUSING ON REALITY, WE
CAUGHT UP IN OUR DREAMS.
HOW WE WANT THINGS TO BE, COMPARED TO
HOW IT REALLY IS.
AFFAIRS CAN BE DECEITFUL, IF YOU AREN'T
APART OF THE BIZ.
BELIEVE HALF OF WHAT YOU PERCEIVE, AND
NONE OF WHAT YOU HEAR.
MATTERS CAN BE FALLACIOUS, TO MAKE YOU
SEEM INSINCERE.
THE DEVIL USES WEAK PEOPLE, SO KEEP THEM
FAKE PEOPLE FROM AROUND YOU.
SO DEVIOUS, IN GOD PRESENTS THEY STILL
CAN'T BE TRUE.
EVEN THOUGH WHAT IT SEEMS LIKE, WHAT IT
IS BUT IT AIN'T.
THE DEVIL LOOKS HOLY, THE ONE LOOK LIKE
A THUG BE A SAINT.
YOUR EYES WANT BELIEVE WHAT YOUR MIND
CAN'T PERCEIVE.
IF YOU DON'T DO YOUR OWN RESEARCH,
YOU'LL ALWAYS BE DECEIVE.

MISLEADING BECAUSE THE TRUTH HURT, AND
THEY WANT TO LIVE A LIE.
CONVERTING YOUR SPIRITUALITY TO
RELIGION, WORSHIPPING A MAN IN THE SKY.
DISTORTED YOUR HISTORY, DON'T KNOW
WHERE YOU COME FROM OR GOING.
THE DEVIL IS THE MASTER OF DECEPTION,
HAVE FAITH IN THE ALL-KNOWING.

HANDLE MY BIZ

I'M NOT TURNING THE OTHER CHEEK; I'M
AIMING STRAIGHT AT YOUR DOME.
THE SAME CONDITION I LEFT; I'M MAKING IT
BACK HOME.
THEY SMILE IN YOUR FACE, AND STAB YOU IN
THE BACK.
NOW YOU DEAD WRONG WHEN YOU RECOVER,
AND THEN HAVE THEM WACK.
NOW I STAY SOLO, BECAUSE I DON'T TRUST A
SOUL.
THE THINGS THAT I BEEN THROUGH GOT MY
HEART ICE COLD.
FOOLS WILL HATE YOU FOR DOING BETTER,
INSTEAD OF TRYING TO GET BETTER.
I DON'T DISCRIMINATE MAN, YOU BETTER
COME GET HER.
IT'S ALL-OUT WARFARE, WHEN MY FREEDOM &
LIFE ON THE LINE.

TO MANY TIMES I BEEN MISLED BY MY HEART,
I'M FOLLOWING MY MIND.
WHEN THE TABLES TURN, THEY WANT TO PLAY
VICTIM.
THEY WERE BAD ASS WHEN THEY THOUGHT
YOU WAS SOFT, SURPRISED WHEN YOU
TRICKED THEM.
I HATE GETTING OFF MY PEDESTAL, TO STOOP
TO THESE LOW LEVELS.
IT'S THE ALL MOST HIGH IN ME, I GOT TO
FIGHT THESE DEVILS.
I DON'T HAVE NO TIME TO WASTE, YOU KNOW
WHAT IT IS.
IF IT COME DOWN TO IT, I'M GONE HANDLE MY
BIZ.

MODERN DAY MINSTREL SHOW

WE NO LONGER HAVE THE ONLY OPTION TO
WEAR BLACK FACE, NOW A DAYS WE PUT IT ON
OURSELF.
BLACK PEOPLE VOLUNTARILY SELLING THEY
SOUL, FOR FAME & WEALTH.
ACTING LIKE, LOOKING LIKE, & SOUNDING
LIKE CLOWNS.
REPEATING THE SAME ACTIONS, GENERATIONS
LIKE A MERRY GO ROUND.
TV & RADIO SHOWS, & GOSSIP SITES
DEGRADING OUR OWN PEOPLE.
BUT SOON AS WE GET DONE WRONG BY
ANOTHER RACE, WE WANT TO FIGHT TO BE

EQUAL.
IT'S TOO MUCH IGNORANCE IN OUR MUSIC,
AND OUR MOVIES TOO.
KIDS GROW UP ON IT THINKING IT'S THE
THING TO DO.
THEN THEY TURN AROUND AND BLAME THE
KIDS, FOR THE WAY THAT THEY ACT.
KEEP EXCUSES, BECAUSE IT'S HARD TO FACE
REALITY OR GO BY THE FACTS.
WE NEED A BALANCE OF MORE POSITIVITY, TO
GET OUR SOULS BACK ON TRACK.
AND STOP THINKING IGNORANCE IS COOL,
BECAUSE YOU GOT SOME RACKS.
STOP BEING OXYMORONS, BEING
INTELLIGENTLY LAME.
FIVE MINUTES OF FAME FOR A LIFETIME OF
SHAME.
N!663R DEFINITION USE TO BE IGNORANT, NOW
THEY DEFINE IT AS A BLACK PERSON.
WE NEED TO BETTER OUR RACE BEFORE OUR
SITUATION WORSENS.
YOUR SPIRIT, MORALS, & DIGNITY IS PRICELESS,
IN THE LONG TERM ALWAYS THINK.
STOP BEING MODERN DAY MINSTREL SHOWS,
BEING BAMBOOZLED & HOODWINKED.

WHAT ARE YOU GOING TO DO?

NOW THAT WE HAVE THE KNOWLEDGE, WHAT
ARE YOU GOING TO DO TO MAKE THINGS
IMPROVE.

LIVE RIGHTEOUS SET EXAMPLES TO OTHERS,
ON HOW TO MOVE.
CONTINUE TO SPREAD KNOWLEDGE, TO WAKE
MY BROTHERS AND SISTERS UP.
POSITIVITY INSPIRE THE YOUTH, SO THEY CAN
BE RIGHTEOUS WHEN THEY COME UP.
KEEP MY HEAD UP, CHEST OUT, WILLING TO
DIE FOR WHAT I BELIEVE IN.
IF I DIE CONTINUE TO FIGHT, THERE'S NO TIME
FOR GRIEVING.
ALWAYS STAND FOR SOMETHING OR YOU'D
FALL FOR ANYTHING.
FIGHT THE POWER IS THE ANTHEM, WE ALL
SHOULD SING.
I'LL NEVER BE A FOLLOWER EVEN IF IT'S
TRENDING, I'LL ALWAYS BE A LEADER.
FOR KNOWLEDGE I'LL ALWAYS SEEK & SEARCH,
AND BE A CAREFUL READER.
KEEP MY FAMILY UNITED, WITH A BOND
THAT'S STRONG.
IN THE ATMOSPHERE OF POSITIVE ENERGY, IS
WHERE I'LL ALWAYS BELONG.
I'LL FOREVER SPEAK THE TRUTH, EVEN IF IT
HURT.
I'LL NEVER KNOW IT ALL, SO I'LL KEEP DOING
MY RESEARCH.
STAY PRAYED UP, AND ALWAYS REMAIN
POSITIVE.
IF I HAVE MORE THAN ENOUGH, I'D ALWAYS
GIVE.
NEVER SELL MY SOUL, ALWAYS FIGHT FOR
WHAT'S RIGHT.
NEVER GIVE UP, UNTIL VICTORY IS IN OUR
SIGHT.

HAVE FAITH IN THE ALL MOST HIGH UNTIL MY
LIFE IS THROUGH.
TO MAKE THINGS BETTER, THAT'S WHAT I'M
GOING TO DO.

HAPPY BIRTHDAY MOM

HAPPY BIRTHDAY MOM, I LOVE AND MISS YOU.
I WISH I WASN'T SO FAR AWAY; I WISH I WAS
THERE WITH YOU.
I HOPE YOU ENJOYED YOUR DAY.
HOW I'M FEELING, I HOPE I CAN FIND THE
WORDS TO SAY.
IT HURT ME THAT I WAS ON LOCKDOWN,
UNABLE TO CALL.
YOU ARE IN MY PRAYER'S NIGHT AND DAILY,
TO THE MOST HIGH THE ALL.
I'LL BE HOME SOON, TO MAKE UP FOR THE
LOST TIME.
THEY TRYING TO TAKE MY LIFE, KNOWING I
DIDN'T DO THE CRIME.
IT'S ONE OF THOSE DAYS, I'M TRYING TO HOLD
BACK TEARS.
KNOWING IN THE FUTURE, WE WILL HAVE
BETTER YEARS.
I THANK YOU FOR MY LIFE AND EVERYTHING
THAT YOU DONE.
TO ME YOU ARE THE BEST MOM, YOU'LL
ALWAYS BE NUMBER ONE.
KEEP YOUR HEAD UP, STAY PRAYED UP, AND

ALWAYS THINK THE BEST.
WHEN I COME BACK, YOU'LL NEVER HAVE TO
SETTLE FOR LESS.
THE FEELING THAT I'M FEELING, I HOPE THESE
WORDS DISPLAY.
I LOVE YOU & MISS YOU MOM, HAPPY
BIRTHDAY.

THE ALL MOST HIGH

THE REASON WHY I WAKE UP EVERY MORNING,
FEELING SO BLESSED.
THE ALL ANSWER MY PRAYS, EVERY TIME I'M
FEELING STRESSED.
WITHOUT THE MOST HIGH, I'D PROBABLY BEEN
GIVING UP OR DEAD.
THE ALL KEEP ME FOCUS, BECAUSE SHE HAS
BETTER PLANS INSTEAD.
I FEEL CHOSEN, BECAUSE ALL THESE DEVIL
PLOTS & SCHEMES.
I ALWAYS COME OUT ON TOP, THE MOST HIGH
REIGN SUPREME.
I'M JUST THE VESSEL, THE ALL WORKS
THROUGH ME.
I DON'T TAKE CREDIT FOR NONE; I GIVE THE
MOST HIGH GLORY.
IT'S BEEN PLENTY OF TIMES, WHEN I THOUGHT
I WAS OVER & DONE.
I FIND A WAY TO RISE & SHINE, LIKE I'M GOD
SUN.

THEY LAUGH NOW, CRY LATER, BECAUSE THE
ALL IS GREATER.
THE MOST HIGH ELEVATE ME TO THE TOP,
LIKE I'M ON AN ESCALATOR.
POSITIVE SPIRIT AND SOUL, AND MY MINDS
STRESS FREE.
POSITIVE VIBRATIONS, FREQUENCIES, AND
ENERGY.
IF YOU CAN THINK AND DREAM IT, YOU CAN
DO IT, IF YOU APPLY.
AND STAY IN TUNE WITH THE MIGHTY ALL
MOST HIGH.

MY HEART STILL WORK

IN A TIME OF UNKNOWING, MY KNOWLEDGE &
FAITH KEEP GROWING.
AT TIMES IT DOES BE HARD, BUT I'M NEVER
SHOWING.
I STAYED PRAYED UP, KEEP MY HEAD UP, AND
MY CHEST POKED OUT.
KNOWING IF IT'S MEANT TO BE, IT WILL BE
WITHOUT A DOUBT.
DIAMONDS ARE FORMED FROM BEING UNDER
PRESSURE.
KEEP YOUR SPIRIT STRONG, THE DEVIL WILL
CONTINUALLY TEST YA.
ONE DAY IT'LL BE ALL OVER, AND WE WILL SIT
BACK AND LAUGH.
UNLESS SATAN CORRUPT YOU, AND YOU
CHOOSE THE WRONG PATH.
IF YOU NEVER LEARN THE LESSON, YOU'LL
CONTINUED TO BE TEST.

IF YOUR HEART ISN'T PURE, YOU'LL NEVER BE
BLESSED.
MAYBE TEMPORARILY WITH EARTHLY
POSSESSIONS, YOU CAN'T DIE WITH THEM.
NOW YOUR SOUL CAN'T TRANSCEND, AND YOU
ARE STUCK IN THIS REALM.
MY VOLTAGE STAYS HIGH, SO I CAN MOVE
BEYOND THIS DIMENSION.
I DON'T BE AROUND NEGATIVE PEOPLE, I'M
ALLERGIC TO TENSION.
MY HEART STILL WORKS, AFTER IT'S BEEN
STABBED, STEPPED ON, AND BROKE.
I STILL SHOW LOVE, AFTER I BEEN PROVOKED.

MY FANTASTIC FIVE

IT'S SO HARD BEING AWAY FROM MY KIDS, I
LOVE THEM SO MUCH.
I MISS HEARING THEY VOICE, AND BEING ABLE
TO REACH OUT AND TOUCH.
I PRAY FOR THEM DAY & NIGHT, CONTINUALLY.
ASKING TO BLESS THEM AND LET THEM KNOW,
I LOVE THEM INSINUALLY.
TWO SONS AND THREE DAUGHTERS, THE
WONDERS OF MY WORLD.
THERE'S NOTHING I WOULDN'T DO FOR THEM,
IN THIS WORLD.
MY TWO BOYS DONE BECAME MEN, I SO PROUD
OF THEM.

IN THIS PREJUDICE WORLD, PRAY THEY NEVER
BECOME A VICTIM.
MY DAUGHTERS I HOPE THEY FIND THE GOD
IN THEM, TO GROW UP AND BE QUEENS.
AND DON'T GET CAUGHT UP IN THE ENTICING
AGES BEING A TEEN.
I'M TRYING MY HARDEST TO GET BACK IN
THEIR LIFE, WHERE I BELONG.
TO CREATE A BOND, EVERLASTING,
ETERNALLY STRONG.
I KNOW THE ALL MOST HIGH GOING TO WORK
IT OUT AND FIND AWAY.
BECAUSE AFTER EVERY STORM, THEY ARE
ALWAYS BRIGHTER DAYS.
ANYTHING THEY NEED FROM ME, WHILE I'M
ALIVE.
THEY CAN GET IT ANYTIME, MY FANTASTIC
FIVE.

DEMONIAC SPIRITS

ONCE YOU CROSS CERTAIN LINES, THEIRS IS NO
EVER COMING BACK.
OUR RELATIONSHIP DIMINISHED; IT'LL NEVER
BE INTACT.
EVEN IF WE TRY TO REKINDLE IT, IT'LL NEVER
BE THE SAME.
SOME THINGS ARE BETTER OFF NOT BEING,
LIFE ISN'T A GAME.
SOME PEOPLE THINK THE WORLD REVOLVE
AROUND THEM, AND THEY GOT ALL THE

SENSE.
BUT THEY ONLY BE FOOLING THEMSELVES,
BECAUSE THEY ARE SO DENSE.
LESS PEOPLE, LESS PROBLEMS, MOST OF THE
TIMES YOU ARE BETTER OFF BY YOURSELF.
DON'T LOOK FOR FAVORS, PAY FOR THE
SERVICE, OR DO IT YOURSELF.
SOME PEOPLE AREN'T SATISFIED, UNTIL THEY
SEE YOU DOWN & OUT.
NO MATTER HOW MANY TIMES YOU WERE
THERE FOR THEM, THEY RATHER SEE YOU
WITHOUT.
I'M BLESSED MY VALIDATION COMES FROM THE
ALL, & NOT MAN.
BECAUSE PEOPLE WILL FAIL YOU EVERY TIME,
NOT STICKING TO THE PLAN.
THEY ARE EITHER POSSESSED. LOST, OR JUST
SOULLESS BEINGS.
ONLY A CASKET, DEBT, OR TROUBLE, THEY
WANT TO SEE YOU IN.
RIGHTEOUSNESS AND THE TRUTH, THEY CAN'T
STAND TO HEAR IT.
STAY FOCUS AND STAY CLEAR OF THESE
DEMONIAC SPIRITS.

YOU ARE APPRECIATED

DEAR QUEEN, HOW ARE YOU DOING? ME I
TRULY MISS YOU.
I APPRECIATE YOU BEING HERE FOR ME, &
EVERYTHING THAT YOU DO.

I NEVER WOULD OF IMAGINE BEING IN THIS
SITUATION.
SEEING YOU AGAIN, I HAVE SO MUCH
ANTICIPATION.
THEY SAY THINGS HAPPEN FOR A REASON, ONE
DAY IT WILL ALL MAKE SENSE.
SOME THINGS THAT HAPPEN IN OUR LIFE,
HAVE US IN SO MUCH SUSPENSE.
LUCKILY, WE GOT TO SPEND TIME, BEFORE I
WAS TAKING AWAY.
SEEM LIKE I BEEN GONE FOR FOREVER, AND A
DAY.
TELL LIL MAN I SAID WHAT'S UP, AND I MISS HIM
TOO.
FEEL LIKE I OWE YOU MY LIFE, THERE'S
NOTHING IN THIS WORLD I WOULDN'T DO FOR
YOU.
YOUR WORDS OF INSPIRATION, KEEP ME
FOCUSED AND GROUNDED.
I CAN'T WAIT TO SEE YOUR FACE AGAIN; I'LL BE
SO ASTOUNDED.
GOING THROUGH THESE ROUGH TIMES, ONLY
MAKE OUR RELATIONSHIP STRONGER.
I HOPE THIS PROCESS BE OVER SOON, AND WE
DON'T HAVE TO WAIT MUCH LONGER.
GOING THROUGH THIS SITUATION, ONLY
MADE MY LOVE UPGRADED.
I LOVE YOU AND I THANK YOU; YOU ARE
APPRECIATED.

NEVER GIVE UP

IT ISN'T OVER, UNTIL ALL THE TIME HAS
EXPIRED.
UNLESS YOU GRACEFULLY BOW OUT, OR YOU
RETIRED.
KNOWING IN YOUR HEART AND MIND, YOU
GAVE IT YOUR ALL.
NEVER GIVE UP AND SETTLE FOR THE FALL.
ALWAYS KNOW IF THERE'S A WILL, THERE'S A
WAY.
WHEN THINGS SEEM TO HARD, CALL ON THE
ALL MOST HIGH AND PRAY.
THE ALL WILL ALWAYS MAKE A WAY FOR YOU.
THERE'S NOTHING IN THIS WORLD, IF YOU
DON'T APPLY YOURSELF YOU CAN'T DO.
BLOCK OUT ALL THE NEGATIVE, AND
UNAMBITIOUS ABOMINATIONS.
MAKE THIS WORLD A BETTER PLACE, FOR THE
FUTURE GENERATIONS.
JUST KEEP GOING HARD, UNTIL YOU LOSE
YOUR BREATHE.
UNTIL YOU KNOW YOU GAVE IT YOUR ALL,
AND THERE IS NOTHING LEFT.
NEVER DWELL ON THE PROBLEM, ALWAYS
SEEK THE SOLUTION.
JUST KEEP WORKING HARD, UNTIL YOU REACH
A RESOLUTION.
IF YOU ARE UP THEN FALL DOWN, COME BACK
UP LIKE A CUP.
ALWAYS KNOW YOU CAN, AND NEVER GIVE UP.

KINDNESS FOR WEAKNESS

SOME PEOPLE THINK BECAUSE YOU ARE
CARING, AND SHOW LOVE ALL THE TIME.
THEY DON'T WANT TO SEE YOU EVOLVE; THEY
WANT YOU STUCK IN YOUR PRIME.
THEY CAN'T ACCEPT THE LOVE; THEY PUSH IT
UNTIL YOU SET THEM STRAIGHT.
THEN WHEN YOU TELL THEM ABOUT
THEMSELVES, THEY SAY WHY YOU WANT TO
HATE.
SCHEMERS AND CONS WILL GO FAR AND
BEYOND.
DOING RIGHT IS A SIN, BECAUSE THEY ARE
DEMONS.
WILL GO AS FAR AS TRYING TO DECEIVE WITH
RELIGION, TALKING BUT NOT LIVING IT.
ALWAYS BEGGING WITH THEIR HANDS OUT,
BUT YOU NEVER SEE THEM GIVING IT.
LEARNING NOT TO REACT, IS THE HARDEST
LESSON OF ALL
SOME PEOPLE ARE ONLY HERE TO SET YOU UP
FOR THE FALL.
NEVER LET NO ONE TAKE YOU OUT OF
CHARACTER OR ANGER YOU.
THINK BEFORE YOU ACT BE CONSCIOUS OF
THE THINGS THAT YOU DO.
EVERY CAUSE HAS ITS EFFECT, AND EVERY
EFFECT HAS ITS CAUSE.
EVERYTHING HAPPENS ACCORDING TO THE
NATURE OF THE LAWS.
THE ALL MOST HIGH BLESSINGS, YOU SHOULD
SEEK THIS.

BELIEVE IN TOUGH LOVE OR GET YOUR
KINDNESS TOOK FOR WEAKNESS.

MY DAUGHTER SWEET SIXTEEN

8-13-21

IT'S SO HARD BEING AWAY ON MY FIRST
DAUGHTER BIRTHDAY.
I MISS TAKING YOU TO THE PARK, JUST TO SEE
YOU PLAY.
I'VE WATCHED YOU GROW UP RIGHT BEFORE
MY EYES.
WE HAVE A BOND UNBREAKABLE, FATHER AND
DAUGHTER TIES.
YOU WILL ALWAYS BE MY PRINCESS, BUT YOU
ARE BECOMING A QUEEN.
NOW I HAVE TO FIGHT AWAY THESE BOYS,
SINCE YOU ARE A MATURE TEEN.
YOU ARE A LEO LIKE ME, SO WE ARE TWO OF A
KIND.
I WISH LIFE HAD A BUTTON, SO I COULD HIT
REWIND.
BUT I CAN'T TURN BACK THE HANDS OF TIMES,
SO I'LL ENJOY THE PRESENT.
I WISH I WAS THERE FOR YOU, SO I COULD GIVE
YOU A PRESENT.
IN DUE TIME, I'LL BE HOME SOON.

TO BE THERE FOR YOU , SO OUR MEMORIES
CAN RESUME.

I HOPE YOU HAVE A GREAT TIME, AND ENJOY
YOUR DAY.
I HOPE YOUR BIRTHDAY WISH COME TRUE AND
EVERYTHING GO YOUR WAY.
I'M A VERY PROUD FATHER, WATCHING YOU
GROW FROM A BABY TO A TEEN.
I LOVE YOU SINCERELY JANAYA, HAPPY SWEET
SIXTEEN.

SHAKE IT OFF

I'M FEELING DOWN AND NOT GOOD, BUT I GOT
TO KEEP ON PUSHING.
THEY HOPING I'M OUT FOR THE COUNT, BUT
TELL THEM KEEP ON WISHING.
DEATH IS THE ONLY THING THAT CAN STOP
ME, FROM REACHING MY DESTINY.
BEING UNDER PRESSURE, ONLY BRINGS OUT
THE BEST IN ME.
I'M GOING THROUGH A TRANSITION, BUT I'M
GOING TO TURN OUT ASTONISH.
IT MIGHT BE HARD TIMES NOW, BUT IN THE
END WE GOING TO BE A BLISS.
ALL I GOT TO DO IS STAY FOCUS, KEEP FAITH,
AND MAINTAIN.
KEEP MY ENERGY POSITIVE, AVOID DEVILS,
AND REMAIN SANE.
I KNOW SATAN STAY BUSY, BUT HE'LL NEVER
DECEIVE ME.
THE ALL MOST HIGH MADE ME, HE'LL ALWAYS
PERCEIVE ME.
FROM A BOY TO A MAN, NOW I'M FEELING
GODLY.

WE'LL NEVER BE EVEN, BECAUSE I'M SO
ODDLY.
I KEEP MY THIRD EYE OPEN, AND MY CHAKRAS
ALIGN.
STAY IN TUNE WITH THE LAWS OF NATURE, SO
I'LL ALWAYS BE FINE.
THE MOST HIGH IS IN ME, I CAN NEVER BE
SOFT.
THE DEVIL TRY HARD TO GET AT ME, BUT I
SHAKE HIM OFF.

JEALOUS HEARTED

ENVY, THE POISON, SEEPS DEEP IN YOUR CORE,
YOUR HATE IS SO OBVIOUS, IT'S HARD TO
IGNORE.
BURNING WITH DESIRE, CONSUMING YOU
MORE.
PLOTTING ON MY DOWNFALL, SEEM LIKE YOUR
CHORE.
FORBIDDEN FRUITS, YOU WATCH OTHERS
ENJOY,
A GROWN MAN, WITH EMOTIONS OF A BOY.
AS YOU DROWN IN THIS SEA OF BITTER ALLOY.
NOTHING YOU CAN DO, WILL STEAL MY JOY.
GREEN-TINGED SPECTACLES CLOUD YOUR
SIGHT,
IF YOU FOCUSED ON BETTERING YOURSELF,
YOU'D BE ALRIGHT.
ENVY WHISPERS, TORMENTING DAY AND
NIGHT.
I'M TO ENLIGHTEN, YOU CAN DIM MY LIGHT.

YEARNING FOR WHAT YOU LACK, WHAT
OTHERS HOLD,
YOUR INSECURITIES, GOT YOUR HEART SO
COLD.
THIS IS THE ALL MOST HIGH GIVEN, WHAT I
BEHOLD.
YOUR STUCK IN A PRISON OF ENVY, WITH A
STORY UNTOLD.

FOCUS

YOU CAN'T LOSE SITE OF YOUR PURPOSE, YOU
GOT TO KEEP YOUR EYES ON THE PRIZE.
THEY'LL CONTINUALLY TRY TO SET YOU UP
FOR FAILURE, YOU CAN'T LET NOTHING STOP
YOU TO RISE.
THE DEVIL WILL TRY TO PLANT SEEDS OF
DESTRUCTION IN YOUR MIND.
DON'T GET DETOURED, DON'T LET NOTHING
TAKE YOU OFF YOUR GRIND.
STAY AWARE, DECEPTIVE SOULS WILL TRY TO
TRICK YOU OUT YOUR SPOT.
MAD BECAUSE YOU ARE DOING GOOD, AND
YOU ARE SOMETHING THAT THEY ARE NOT.
THE MASTER OF DECEPTION, CONTROLLER OF
SOULLESS BEINGS.

SATAN HIMSELF, IF IT'S SOME EVIL GOING ON
BEST BELIEVE INVOLVED HE'S IN.
BUT WHEN THE ALL MOST HIGH IS WITH YOU,
THERE IS NO CONTEST.
ANYTHING YOU ARE INVOLVED IN, GIVE IT
YOUR ALL DO YOUR BEST.

WHAT'S FOR YOU, IF YOU TRY, IT WILL SURELY
BE.
ALWAYS STAY FOCUS, EVEN IF IT'S HARD TO
SEE.
NEVER LET A DECEIVER, TRY TO BLUR YOUR
PERCEPTION.
BY ANY MEANS NECESSARY, WITHOUT NO
EXCEPTION.
THEY'LL TRY TO GET AT YOU IN ALL WAYS,
EVEN TAUNT US OR JOKE US.
JUST REMEMBER KEEP YOUR SPIRIT HIGH,
FAITH STRONG, AND ALWAYS STAY FOCUS.

UNDERSTANDING

SOME THINGS WE GO THROUGH IN LIFE, IS
BEYOND OUR UNDERSTANDING.
EVEN IF YOU WALKING A STRAIGHT PATH, AND
HAVE RIGHTEOUS PLANNING.
YOUR VERY DOWNFALL, MIGHT BE THE
REASON OF A GREAT UPRISING.
THE SAME PEOPLE THAT HATE, NOW YOU
HAVE THEM SYMPATHIZING.
LIKE AL KHIDR TOLD MOSES, YOU WILL NOT BE
ABLE TO HAVE PATIENCE WITH ME.
THE ACTIONS SEEM BAD NOW, BUT IN THE
FUTURE THE DEEDS WILL BE GREATLY.
IF YOU ARE ONLY FOCUSED ON THE ONGOING,
YOU CAN'T FORESEE THE HEREAFTER.
THINGS THAT MAKE YOU CRY NOW,
EVENTUALLY WILL BRING YOU LAUGHTER.

REMAIN POSITIVE AND ENLIGHTEN, AND
FOLLOW THE ALL PLAN.
STAY FOCUS AND AWARE, AND YOUR HORIZON
WILL EXPAND.
FOR SITUATIONS BEYOND YOUR
UNDERSTANDING, ALWAYS KEEP FAITH.
THE ALL MOST HIGH KNOW YOUR HEART, AND
WILL STILL TEST YOUR FAITH.
IT COULD BE SO SIMPLE, BUT WE RATHER MAKE
IT HARD.
IS IT THE LIFE WE CHOOSE, OR WE ARE JUST
PLAYING OUR BEST CARD.
ANYTHING THAT'S GOOD YOU WILL
GRAVITATE TOWARDS, IT WOULDN'T HAVE TO
BE DEMANDING.
KEEPING YOUR EYES OPEN PAY ATTENTION,
AND YOU WILL EVENTUALLY HAVE
UNDERSTANDING.

PHASE VI

ENLIGHTEN

P.U.S.H. (PRAY UNTIL SOMETHING HAPPEN)

I PRAY TO STAY FOCUS, & EASE MY MIND.
I PRAY TO MAINTAIN, & STAY ON MY GRIND.
I PRAY FOR ALL THE GOOD IN MY LIFE, &
BLESSING.
I PRAY TO BE AWARE TO LEARN A LESSON.
I PRAY FOR BETTER DAYS, WITHOUT STRESSING.
I PRAY TO BLOCK THE DEVIL, WHILE HE
TESTING.
I PRAY FOR THE FAMILY AND FRIENDS IN MY
LIFE.
I PRAY FOR THOSE WHO TRY TO STAB ME IN
THE BACK WITH A KNIFE.
I PRAY FOR BEING BLESSED TO SEE ANOTHER
DAY.
I PRAY TO BE RIGHTEOUS AND BE LEAD TO GO
THE RIGHT WAY.
I PRAY FOR POSITIVE VIBRATIONS AND
ENERGY.
I PRAY TO BE THE BEST I CAN BE.
I PRAY TO BE ABLE TO FULFILL MY DESTINY.
I PRAY TO NEVER LET THE WICKED GET THE
BEST OF ME.
I PRAY TO SPEAK THE TRUTH WITHOUT NO
CAPPING.
I PRAY, I PRAY UNTIL SOMETHING HAPPEN.

THE WRATH OF CUE

IT ISN'T OVER, I WILL RETURN , THE WRATH OF
CUE.
THEY SHOWED ME THEY TRUE COLORS, AND

IT'S HUE.

THE ALL GIVE IT'S TOUGHEST BATTLE, TO HER STRONGEST PEOPLE.

DEATH IS THE ONLY THING THAT COULD STOP ME, YOU'LL NEVER SEE ME FOLD.

EVEN THOUGH IT MIGHT HURT, THE TRUTH GOT TO BE TOLD.

I'M SO ENLIGHTEN, I'M LIKE SUN RAYS SHINING ON THE GOLD.

I'M ON MY QUEST TO FULFILL MY DESTINY.

YOU HAD YOUR CHANCE AND BLEW IT, NOW THERE'S NO STOPPING ME.

I'M COMING BACK LOOKING AND FEELING LIKE A NEW MAN.

IF THE THOUGHT COME TO MY MIND, I KNOW THAT I CAN.

I DON'T GET MAD, NOR DO I GET EVEN.

I JUST STAY FOCUS, AND HAVE FAITH IN WHO I BELIEVE IN.

I'LL STICK TO THE SCRIPT, OUT OF SIGHT OUT OF MIND.

TAKE CARE OF MY FAMILY, AND STAY ON MY GRIND.

FAILURES NO OPTION, I'M RISING TO THE TOP.

IF YOU AREN'T FOR ME OR WITH ME, I SEE YOU AS A OP.

MY BABY BOY II A MAN
8-24-21

HAPPY 20TH BIRTHDAY TO MY BABY BOY,
THAT'S NOW A MAN.
I KNOW YOU ARE GOING TO FULFILL YOUR

DESTINY, THAT GOD PLAN.
IT HURT ME THAT I CAN'T BE THERE WITH YOU.
WHEN I GET HOME, WE GOT SOME MAKING UP
TO DO.
I HOPE YOU ENJOY YOUR DAY, AND GET
EVERYTHING YOU WISH.
I CAN'T WAIT TO GO BACK TO JUBILEE, AND
EAT YOUR FAMOUS DISH.
I STILL CAN'T BELIEVE MY BABY BOY IS NOW A
MAN.
I REMEMBER YOUR FIRST BIRTHDAY, WHEN I
DRESSED UP AS SPIDER-MAN.
I REMEMBER STAYING UP WITH YOU
WATCHING SHREK BACK TO BACK.
I WISH I COULD HIT REWIND, AND TURN THE
TIME BACK.
BUT NOW YOU ARE YOUNG MAN, TIME DO FLY.
WITH THE WHOLE WORLD AHEAD OF YOU, THE
LIMIT IS THE SKY.
YOU ARE AWESOME SON, I AM A VERY PROUD
DAD.
I CHERISH EVERY MOMENT, ALL THE PRICELESS
TIME THAT WE HAD.
YOU'RE A HANDSOME YOUNG FELLA, SOON TO
BE IN HIGH DEMAND.
GOD BLESS MY BABY BOY, THAT'S NOW TURN
INTO MAN.

SUPER SAIYAN SON

DREAM BIG, MY SON, FOR YOU HOLD THE KEY,
WHATEVER YOU PUT YOUR MIND TO, YOU CAN
BE.

TO UNLOCK DOORS OF POSSIBILITY.
NOTHING EXCEEDS YOU CAPABILITY.
WITH STRENGTH AND PASSION, LET YOUR
SPIRIT SOAR,
YOU CAN DICTATE THE FUTURE, YOU CAN'T
CHANGE THE BEFORE.
HAVE FAITH & BELIEVE IN YOURSELF, FOREVER
MORE.
NEGATIVE ENERGY AND VIBRATIONS, ALWAYS
IGNORE.
NO LIMITS EXIST WHEN YOU SET YOUR AIM,
MANIFEST YOUR DESTINY, VICTORY IS YOUR TO
PROCLAIM.
UNLEASH YOUR POWER, KINDLE YOUR OWN
FLAME.
BELIEVE IN YOURSELF, SO THEIRS NO ONE
ELSE TO BLAME.
EMBRACE THE JOURNEY, LET YOUR DREAMS
TAKE FLIGHT,
FAILURES NOT AN OPTION WHEN YOU APPLY
ALL YOUR MIGHT.
STAY DISCIPLINE AND FOCUS, ALWAYS DO
WHAT'S RIGHT.
FOR WITH DETERMINATION, YOU'LL REACH
GREAT HEIGHTS

THE GOOD GO UNHEARD

THIS IS FOR ALL THE MELANATED MEN,
HANDLING THEY BUSINESS DOING RIGHT.
WHO NEVER GET THE CREDIT THEY DESERVE,

AS IF WE ARE OUT OF SIGHT.
OUR ACTIONS SHOULD SPEAK LOUDER THAN
WORDS, BUT THEY ONLY ADDRESS THE BAD.
LIKE THE FALSE PERCEPTION, THAT BLACK
MEN AREN'T GOOD DADS.
YOU CAN DO A MILLION RIGHTS, AND THEY
STILL LOOK FOR ONE WRONG.
TO PLACE YOU IN A CATEGORY, WHERE YOU
DON'T BELONG.
REAL MEN GOING TO HANDLE THEY BUSINESS,
DESPITE GETTING ANY GLORY.
WE AREN'T LOOKING FOR ANY REWARDS, THIS
IS FOR MY FAMILY NOT FOR ME.
SOME DO FALL VICTIM TO THE STEREOTYPE
AND PROPAGANDA.
WE KNOW SATAN IS DECEIVING, BUT WE GOT
TO STOP HIS PLAN BRAH.
IF THE GOOD GOT PRESS LIKE THE BAD,
THEY'LL BE NO CONTEST.
THEY SHOULD COUNT THE GRADUATES AND
ACHIEVERS, LIKE THEY DO THE ARREST.
A MAJORITY WHITE CITY, WITH MOSTLY BLACKS
IN JAIL.
IS THIS MODERN DAY JIM CROW, OR WE LIVING
IN HELL.
MAJORITY OF MELANATED MEN IS GREAT,
DON'T BE ABSURD.
WE'LL CONTINUE TO TAKE CARE OF OUR
FAMILIES AND COMMUNITIES, THE GOOD GO
UNHEARD.

CUE INTUITION

UNLIKE KING SOLOMON I HAD ZERO WIFE'S, &
SEVERAL CONCUBINES.
IT WASN'T MY CHOICE, I WAS WILLING TO MAKE
THEM MINE.
MINE, TO MYSELF OR MY WIFE AT ONE POINT, I
WANTED THEM ALL TO BE.
THEY ACT LIKE I WAS THE PLAYER, WHEN THEY
RAN OUT ON ME.
ME, IS THE ONLY PERSON I CAN DEPEND ON,
I'M BETTER OFF BY MYSELF.
I'M NOT TRYING TO TEMPORARILY BALL, I'M
TRYING TO BUILD WEALTH.
WEALTH CAN'T STOP DEATH, UNLESS WEALTH
IS YOUR HEALTH.
ALWAYS REMAIN FOCUS, MOVE REAL STEALTH.
STEALTH IS RARE NOWADAYS, CAUSE
EVERYONE WANT TO POST, SHARE, AND
TWEET.
FROM PEOPLE AND THEY WORLDLY WAYS I
BECOME DISCRETE.
DISCRETE FROM THESE DEVILS, DEMONS, AND
FOOLS.
AUTHORITIES IN THIS COUNTRY, DON'T
FOLLOW THEY OWN RULES.
RULE NUMBER ONE, FOLLOW YOUR FIRST
INSTINCT.
BE YOURSELF, HAVE YOUR OWN IDENTITY SO
YOU'LL BE DISTINCT.
DISTINCT, TO THE WORLD, THAT I'M
ENLIGHTEN AND BLESS.
THESE ARE MY TESTIMONIES, SO I MUST
CONFESS.

BEFORE LEAVING EARTH

I PRAY I CAN MAKE MY MOM HAPPY, AND BE
THERE FOR HER UNTIL THE END.
I WANT TO SEE ALL MY FAMILY TOGETHER,
CLOSE AND EXTEND.
I PRAY THAT I CAN PAY MY SISTER BACK, FOR
ALL SHE DONE FOR ME.
I PRAY THAT MY KIDS GROW UP TO BE ALL
THEY CAN BE.
I PRAY TO REDEEM MYSELF, AND RIGHT ALL MY
WRONGS.
I PRAY TO FULFILL MY DESTINY, AND END UP
WHERE I BELONG.
I PRAY THAT MY LEGACY INSPIRE THE NEXT
GENERATION.
I PRAY THAT MY POEMS HELP BUILD UP A
NATION.
I PRAY TO BE RICH IN SOUL, AND WEALTHY IN
SPIRIT.
AND TOUCH EVERY ONE HEART, THAT SEE ME
OR HEAR IT.
I PRAY TO MAKE MY SEEDS HAPPY, BEING THE
BEST DAD I CAN BE.
AND THE BLOODLINE CONTINUE TO GROW
STRONG, THROUGH THEM, TO THE NEXT
GENERATION, UNTIL ETERNITY.
I PRAY THAT I CAN INSPIRE THEM TO EAT
HEALTHY, TO LIVE LONG.
I PRAY THAT MY LIFE DON'T BE ANOTHER SAD

SONG.
I PRAY THANKING THE ALL MOST HIGH FOR
BEING THERE FOR ME SINCE MY BIRTH.
I PRAY TO BE ACCOMPLISHED, PLUS MORE
BEFORE LEAVING EARTH.

LIVE AND YOU LEARN

A LIE CAN MAKE IT AROUND THE WORLD,
BEFORE THE TRUTH PUT IT'S SHOES ON.
MOST OF THE PEOPLE THAT WANT TO BE THE
FIRST TO SAY AND DO, WITHOUT RESEARCH BE
DEAD WRONG.
IF YOU ARE LOOKING FOR VALIDATION AND
ACCEPTANCE FROM MAN INSTEAD OF THE ALL.
YOU ARE IN FOR A MISERABLE LIFE, SETTING
YOURSELF UP FOR THE FALL.
THIS TO SHALL PAST, YOU SHOULD LIVE YOUR
LIFE TO EVER LAST.
TAKE YOUR TIME DO IT RIGHT, EVERYTHING
DON'T COME FAST.
EASY COME EASY GO, IS A LIFE LESSON MOTTO.
PLAN AND STRATEGIZE AND EVEN PLOT MORE.
MONEY OVER EVERYTHING, BECAUSE TIME IS
MONEY.
SOMETIMES IT MIGHT RAIN, BUT IT'S
FOLLOWED BY DAYS THAT'S SUNNY.
THE ENERGY YOU PUT OUT, IS WHAT YOU WILL
RECEIVE, SO ALWAYS BE POSITIVE.
MAKING YOUR LIFE AND OTHERS PEOPLE
LIVES BETTER, IS THE WAY YOU SHOULD LIVE.
WHO EVER CONTROL THE PRESENT, CONTROL
THE PAST.

THE LAST SHALL BE FIRST, AND THE FIRST
SHALL BE LAST.
BE RIGHTEOUSNESS AND UPLIFTING AND
RESPECT YOU'LL EARN.
AND ALWAYS BE AWARE, YOU LIVE AND YOU
LEARN.

BROTHER FROM ANOTHER MOTHER

LIKE BRANCHES ON A TREE WE GROW,
YOU'RE A GREAT FAMILY MAN, & AWESOME
C.E.O.
WE ARE CONNECTED BY A BOND, WE KNOW.
THROUGH MY LIFE TRIALS AND TRIBULATIONS,
YOU OUTGROW.
DIFFERENT MOTHERS, YET BROTHERS WE
BECOME,
HAVING THE SAME VISION CONCERNING
ACTIVISM.
I'M DOWN NOW, BUT FAR FROM BEING DONE.
I THANK YOU FOR THE SUPPORT ON LIFE'S
BATTLES I WON.
THROUGHOUT ALL THE LAUGHTER, AND SHED
TEARS.
ALL AFTER ALL THESE YEARS, WE ARE STILL
HERE.
THROUGH IT ALL, OUR FRIENDSHIP STEERS.
WOUNDS WILL BE HEALED, AFTER THE SMOKE
CLEARS.
I'M FOREVER GRATEFUL, OUR CONNECTION IS
TRUE,
I'D SACRIFICE MY LIFE, IF THAT'S WHAT IT
COMES TO.

I TRULY APPRECIATE EVERYTHING, THAT YOU
DID AND DO.
MY BROTHER FROM ANOTHER MOTHER, I
CHERISH YOU.

DEDICATION TO MY BROTHER REO BOBE
CAIRWELL

IF YOU EVER THOUGHT

I DON'T HAVE NOTHING TOO PROVE, AND I
CAN CARELESS WHAT AN ABOMINATION
THINK.
WE'LL ALWAYS BE INCOMPATIBLE, WE WOULD
NEVER BE IN SYNC.
THEY NEVER HAVE NOTHING TO ARTICULATE,
WHEN YOUR DOING GREAT.
BUT SO MUCH TO VERBALIZE, WHEN THEY
HEAR NEGATIVELY TO SPREAD THE HATE.
I FELT LIKE JESUS CARRYING THE CROSS, AT
LEAST SEVERAL TIMES.
AND IT'S GOING BE ABOUT MY BLOOD, OR
SOME MONEY, IF I EVER COMMIT A CRIME.
WHEN I COME AROUND, THEY HAVE NOTHING
TO SAY.
THEY SAVE THEM LAME AS JOKES, BECAUSE I'M
NOT THE ONE TO PLAY.
I WANT HESITATE TO GO BACK AND LAY
DOWN, FOR STANDING MY GROUND.
KEEP THAT FAKE LOVE, AND HUGS, DAPS, AND
POUNDS.
YA'LL DON'T STAND FOR NOTHING, NEVER
RYDE JUST DIE.

GET CONFRONTED, PLAY SMOKEY, TALKING
ABOUT YOU WAS HIGH.
N!66@$ WITH WHITE DEVILS SOULS, WANT TO
SEE ME DEAD AND GONE.
IT'S GOD GIVEN ALL I GOT TO DO IS SHOW UP,
AND IT'S ON.
THEY NEVER APOLOGIZE OR RECONCILE,
AFTER THEY SEE IT'S B.S. THEY DONE BOUGHT.

YOU WAS NEVER REAL OR KNEW ME, IF YOU
EVER THOUGHT.

YOU PEOPLE

KNOWING IT'S A RACE , WE TO BUSY
COMPETING WITH EACH OTHER.
RACIST AND POLICE KILLING US, AND WE
STEADY KILLING ONE ANOTHER.
ONLY TIME BEING RIGHTEOUS IS ALL RIGHT, IS
WHEN IT'S A MOVEMENT TRENDING.
WITH YOU PEOPLE, I AM NOT TRYING TO
BLEND IN.
JUST LIKE THE BIBLICAL ISRAELITES,
UNGRATEFUL AND UNDISCIPLINED.
DOING THE RIGHT THING TO THEM, SEEM TO
BE A SIN.
QUICK TO KILL EACH OTHER, BUT WANT FIGHT
THE POWER THAT BE.
WHEN THE CONSEQUENCE OF THE LIFESTYLE
KICK IN, THEY MAKE EXCUSES AND PLEA.
I'M FEELING LIKE HOSEA AND GOMER THIRD

CHILD, NOT MY PEOPLE.
THESE UNETHICAL AND MISEDUCATED
NEGROES, ARE NOT MY PEOPLE.
WE GOT INTEGRATED, INSIDE OF A BURNING
HOUSE.
NOW WE ARE MORE SEPARATED, LIKE A
RELATIONSHIP WITH A CHEATING SPOUSE.
THEY PUT MORE FAITH IN THEIR OPPRESSOR,
THAN THEY DO THEY OWN KIND.
THEY GOT TO BE SHOWN AND TOLD
SOMETHING, THEY NEVER USE THEY OWN
MIND.
YOU PEOPLE KNOW UNITED WE STAND, AND
DIVIDED WE FALL.
IF YOU PEOPLE NEVER STAND FOR
SOMETHING, FOR ANYTHING YOU'LL GO FOR IT
ALL.

NOT GOD PLAN (JESUS SAID)

NO MAN CAN'T SERVE TWO MASTERS, YOU
CANNOT SERVE GOD AND MONEY.
YOU DON'T WANT TO PUT IN NO WORK, BUT
ENJOY THE MILK AND HONEY.
YOU HEAR BUT YOU DON'T UNDERSTAND, SEE
BUT YOU CAN'T PERCEIVE.
IDOLIZING FALSE PROPHETS, THE LIFESTYLE
THEY PORTRAY GOT YOU DECEIVE.
THIS CAN'T BE LIFE, LIVING FANTASY ON
SOCIAL MEDIA.
SEE THEM IN REAL LIFE, THEY ALWAYS IN

NEED OF YA.
THE BLIND LEADING THE BLIND, STRAIGHT
INTO A PIT.
BIGGEST ACCOMPLISHMENT IN LIFE IS
PUTTING ON A OUTFITS.
THEY DO A GOOD DEED FOR SOMEONE, THEN
LET THE WORLD KNOW.
DID YOU DO IT FROM THE HEART, OR ALL FOR
SHOW.
ALWAYS SO ANXIOUS TO PRESENT YOUR
CLOTHES, FOOD, AND DRINK.
JESUS SAID IT'S MORE TO LIFE THAN THAT, USE
YOUR MIND AND THINK.
A PROPHET IS WITHOUT HONOR IN HIS
HOMETOWN AND HOUSEHOLD.
WHAT WILL IT PROFIT A MAN TO GAIN THE
WHOLE WORLD, AND LOSE HIS SOUL.
MY GOD, MY GOD, HAVE YOU FORSAKEN US.
WE ALL COME FROM AND WILL RETURN, TO
ASHES TO ASHES AND DUST TO DUST.

THIS ISN'T VANITY

I LOSS A LOT OF TIME, BUT THIS WASN'T
VANITY.
I DISCIPLINED AND EDUCATED MYSELF MORE,
SO A BETTER MAN I CAN BE.
I'M SO FOCUSED, NOTHING CAN STOP ME FROM
REACHING MY DESTINY.
TO OBTAIN MY ZENITH, I'M ON A QUEST TO
SEE.

I'M REJUVENATED, REVIGORATED, AND ABOUT
TO BE RELOCATED.
AND IF YOU HAVE A PROBLEM WITH IT, I
SURELY HATE YOU HATE IT.
I CAN SEE CLEARLY NOW, IT'S EVER SO CLEAR.
IF YOU AREN'T FOR ME, YOU ARE AGAINST ME,
AND I DON'T WANT YOU NEAR.
I'M NOT OF THIS WORLD, ONLY THE ALL MOST
HIGH I FEAR.
HEALING AND POSITIVE FREQUENCIES, IS ALL I
WANT TO HEAR.
I WILL REMEMBER EVERY MOMENT THAT I
BEEN LOCK DOWN.
IF YOU WASN'T HEAR FOR ME DURING THESE
TIMES, I DON'T WANT YOU AROUND.
NAH YOU DON'T OWE ME NOTHING, BUT REAL
PEOPLE DO REAL THINGS.
YOU DON'T WANT TO PUT IN THE HARD WORK,
BUT WANT A CHAMPIONSHIP RING.
I'M GONE SPEAK MY MIND AND STAND MY
GROUND, THAT'S JUST THE MAN IN ME.
ALL THIS WASTED TIME WASN'T SPENT IN
VANITY.

VACCINATED

THEY DON'T CARE ABOUT THE WATER, FOOD,
YOUR WELL BEING, OR THE AIR YOU BREATHE.
BUT I'M SUPPOSED TO TRUST THEM WANTING
TO VACCINATE ME.
ALL THESE EXPERIMENTS THEY PERFORMED
ON CIVILIANS UNKNOWINGLY.

YEARS LATER AFTER IT'S EXPOSED, YOU LUCKY
TO GET A PRESIDENTIAL APOLOGY.
THEY CAUSE THE PROBLEM, THEN COME WITH
THE SOLUTION.
AVOID CLIMATE CONTROL DEBATES, AND
WORLD POLLUTION.
STARTED WITH COVID-19, NOW WE HAVE 12
DIFFERENT VARIANTS.

TO GET VACCINATED HAS BECOME AN
ENABLEMENT.
FROM ALPHA TO OMICRON.
WHAT HAPPENS TO THE OLD VARIANT, WHEN A
NEW ONE COME ALONG.
FULLY VACCINATED WITH A BOOSTER, AND
STILL TEST POSITIVE.
HOW AM I SUPPOSE TO TRUST THEM, AND
REMAIN POSITIVE.
I REFUSE TO FAKE IT LIKE BRETT FARVE &
ANTONIO BROWN, I STAND ON IT LIKE KYRIE.
STAND FOR SOMETHING, OR FALL FOR
ANYTHING, I LOVE ME.
AND I WANT TO KNOW WHAT I'M PUTTING IN
MY BODY, & THE LONG TERM EFFECT.
UNVACCINATED, TWO YEARS LATER AND STILL
HAVE BEEN INFECT..

THE DARK SIDE.

I SHOULD OF LISTENED TO THESE DEMONS, IN
MY HEAD.

MAYBE SOME OF MY OUTCOMES, WOULD OF
CAME OUT BETTER INSTEAD.
HAVING A GOOD HEART, ALWAYS GET YOU
F~<K OVER IN THE END.
IS THERE REALLY A SUCH THING AS AN EVIL
SIN?
SOME PEOPLE SMILE IN YOUR FACE, AND WISH
THE DEATH OF YOU.

ANY NEGATIVELY THAT THEY HEAR, THEY
GOSSIP, NOT KNOWING IF IT'S TRUE.
ALL THE GOOD THAT YOU DONE, DON'T GET
APPRECIATED UNTIL YOU DIE.
THEN THEY ACT AS IF THEY LOVED YOU SO
MUCH, AND IT'S HARD TO SAY GOODBYE.
MY MOTTO ALWAYS BEEN LESS PEOPLE, LESS
PROBLEMS.
BECAUSE DEALING WITH THEM, MY MIND
SWEAR VERY SOLEMN.
UNITED WE STAND, DIVIDED WE FALL.
I TEND TO DO BETTER BY MYSELF, AND NOT
WITH THEM ALL.
THE DEVIL STAY BUSY, GET DOWN OR LAY
DOWN.
YOU ONLY GET ONE LIFE TO LIVE, AND I'M
TRYING TO STICK AROUND.
THEY SAY EVERYTHING COMES TO LIGHT, SO
WHY WASTE YOUR TIME AND HIDE.
I'M ALWAYS TRYING TO ENLIGHT, BUT THIS IS
THE DARK SIDE.

REALITY

I CAN MAKE POEMS ALL DAY & NIGHT, ABOUT
DARK AND HAPPY FEELINGS.
BUT WHEN YOU ADDRESS REALITY, YOU GET
NO REAL DEALINGS.
WE ARE LIVING IN AN AGE OF UNIVERSAL
MIND CONTROL.
PEOPLE TEND TO FOLLOW THE POPULAR,
INSTEAD OF THEIR SOUL.
NEVER THINKING OF THE LONG TERM EFFECT,
IT'S ALL ABOUT NOW.
STAND FOR SOMETHING, YOU FALL FOR
ANYTHING, WHEN YOU TAKE A BOW.
WE ARE NOT PUT HERE TO AGREE ON
EVERYTHING, AND BE THE SAME.
CONTINUING THE SAME ACTIONS, LOOKING
FOR DIFFERENT RESULTS, MAKE YOU LAME.
APOLOGIES WITH NO ACTIONS, WHAT IS IT
WORTH?
WE CAN AGREE TO DISAGREE, AND COEXIST
ON THIS EARTH.
RIGHT IS RIGHT AND WRONG IS WRONG, YOUR
SPIRIT IS AWARE.
OR ARE YOU JUST FOLLOWING A CULT, WITH A
THRONE THAT YOU'D NEVER BE THE HEIR.
IF I'M WRONG LET ME KNOW, I'M ALL ABOUT
BETTERING MYSELF.
IF I'M RIGHT, LEARN FROM ME BETTER
YOURSELF.
LIFE DOESN'T ALWAYS GO THE WAY WE WANT
IT, AND THAT'S HOW IT BE.
BUT IT IS WHAT IT IS, AND WE HAVE TO FACE
REALITY.

KEEP THAT SAME ENERGY

THEY GIVE YOU NO INSPIRATION,
MOTIVATION, OR SUPPORT, WHEN IT'S ALL A
DREAM.
THEN WHEN THE SUCCESS, MONEY, AND FAME
COME, THEY WANT TO BE APART OF YOUR
TEAM.
TRYING TO SPREAD THEY FAKE LOVE AND
LOW VIBRATIONS.
YOU PULL THEM UP, BUT TO PULL YOU DOWN IS
THEY EXPECTATION.
THEY FORGET QUICK, WHEN YOU WAS THERE
AND THEY NEED YOU.
THEY FINALLY GET A LITTLE SOMETHING,
THEN THEY TRY TO BELITTLE YOU.
WHEN YOU ALWAYS HAVE TO BE THE BIGGER
PERSON, YOU DEALING WITH TOO MANY
SMALL PEOPLE.
I ALWAYS CREATED MY OWN WAY, I NEVER
FOLLOW THE SHEEPLE.
THEY LOVE TO CATCH YOU WHILE YOU DOWN,
SO THEY CAN EASILY KICK.
LITTLE DO THEY KNOW STILL I RISE, I'LL BE
BACK UP EASILY QUICK.
KEEP THAT SAME ENERGY, BECAUSE IT'S WEAK
TO ME.
YOU TOO FAR BELOW ME, YOU I CAN'T EVEN
SEE.
IT WAS WRITTEN, THIS IS WHO I WAS CHOOSE
TO BE.
TEN TOES DOWN, CHEST OUT, CHIN UP, I'LL
NEVER FLEE.

YOU HATERS BIRDS OF A FEATHER, WITH THAT
LAME SYNERGY.
IT'S TO LATE TO GET DOWN AND BE COOL,
KEEP THAT SAME ENERGY.

WITH FRIENDS LIKE THESE

YOU AREN'T NO WHERE ON MY MIND, BUT YOU
SO OFFENDED BY MY WORDS.
A HURT DOG HOLLER, NOW YOU ACTING OUT
OF CHARACTER GOING UNHEARD.
IT'S HARD FOR YOU TO LOOK AT YOUR OWN
SELF, SO YOU GET MADE UP.
THAT FANTASY STUFF YOU TALKING, SOUND
ALL MADE UP.
WITH FRIENDS LIKE THESE, WHO NEED
ENEMIES.
INSTEAD OF BEING INSPIRED BY, YOU WANT
ELIMINATE, AND BE ME.
THE SAME THINGS MAKE YOU LAUGH, MAKE
YOU CRY.
LOOK INSIDE YOURSELF, YOU ARE SEVERELY
WOUNDED, SOON TO DIE.
I'M ROYALTY AND YOU ARE NOTHING BUT A
PEASANT.
YOU WERE HIGHLY BLESSED, JUST TO BE IN MY
PRESENCE.
SMILED IN MY FACE, TALKED BEHIND MY BACK.
I HAVE TO DEAL WITH THIS FOOLISHNESS, AND
STAY MENTALLY INTACT.

I AM MY OWN BEING, I IDENTIFY WITH NO
MAN.
I FOLLOW NOBODY AGENDA, I GO WITH GOD
PLAN.
SOMETIMES THE PERSON YOU TAKE A BULLET
FOR, IS STANDING BEHIND THE TRIGGER.
BEING AROUND SMALL MINDED PEOPLE, THAT
CAN'T CONTEMPLATE THAT YOU THINK
BIGGER.
SO YOU MEAN TO TELL ME

SO YOU MEAN TO TELL ME, GOD CREATED THIS
UNIVERSE FOR MAN TO DESTROY?
AND HAVE NO REGARDS FOR ANY OTHER LIFE,
IT'S ALL OURS TO ENJOY.
WE DON'T HAVE OUR OWN AFFAIRS
TOGETHER, BUT WE ARE HERE TO CONTROL
OTHERS.
THEY SAY IT'S A MAN'S WORLD BUT THE
CLOSEST TO GOD IS A MOTHER.
SO YOU MEAN TO TELL ME, THEY CREATED
RELIGION TO KILL YOUR SPIRIT?
YOU ARE MEANT TO DO WHAT YOU ARE TOLD,
INSTEAD OF IF YOU FEEL IT.
TO MAKE IT MORE CONFUSING THEY CREATE
POLITICS.
NEVER LET YOU KNOW WHAT'S GOING ON, ON
YOUR MIND THEY PLAY TRICKS.
SO YOU MEAN TO TELL ME, IT'S MORE
IMPORTANT TO PLEASE MAN AND NOT GOD?
THEY LABEL YOU AS AN OUTCAST, IF YOU GO
AGAINST THE ODDS.
DON'T LET THEM LOWER YOUR VIBRATION,
KILL YOUR SPIRIT, BECAUSE ENERGY NEVER

DIE.
THEY'LL HAVE YOU STUCK IN THE SAME REALM
NOT KNOWING WHY.
SO YOU MEAN TO TELL ME, IT WAS WRITTEN
BUT I HAVE A CHOICE?
IF I TELL THEM THE TRUTH, THEY'LL SILENCE
MY VOICE.
TO MAKE A CHANGE, THAT'S SOMETHING YOU
HAVE TO DIE FOR.

IF IT'S IN THE NAME OF GOD, TO RESOLVE
CONFLICTS WHY WAR?

#NEWYEARSRESOLUTION

IT SHOULDN'T TAKE A NEW YEAR FOR YOU TO
WANT TO CUT OFF YOUR BAD HABITS, BURDENS
& WRONGS.
IF IT WAS THAT EASY TO DO, PEOPLE
WOULDN'T HAVE TO BE SO STRONG.
MOST PEOPLE SOUND LOOPED UP, SAYING THE
SAME THING YEAR AFTER YEAR.
THEY MAKE IT SOUND GOOD, BUT IT'S NEVER
WHAT IT APPEAR.
MIGHT STICK TO IT FOR A WEEK OR TWO, THEN
IT'S BACK TO THE REGULAR SCHEDULE
PROGRAM.
SOME OF THE ACTIONS YOU BEEN DOING FOR
SO LONG, IT TAKE YEARS TO DEPROGRAM.
CUT FRIENDS OFF, STOP SMOKING, LOSE
WEIGHT.
NO SEX, STOP DOING DRUGS, AND GO
STRAIGHT.

BECOME MORE DEDICATED TO YOUR
BUSINESS, START TO WORK OUT.
PRACTICE FOR A COUPLE OF DAYS, IT SEEMS TO
NEVER WORK OUT.
BACK TO LIVING LIKE YOU BEEN LIVING IN
YOUR PREVIOUS YEARS.
BE LIVING THIS WAY FOR SO LONG, YOU MADE
IT A CAREER.

EVERY 24 HOURS YOU GET A NEW DAY.
TAKE IT ONE STEP AT A TIME, YOUR ODDS OF
SUCCEEDING IS BETTER THAT WAY.
IT'S NOTHING WRONG WITH WANTING TO
CHANGE, JUST HAVE A SOLUTION.
YOU'LL HAVE A BETTER CHANCES OF
ACCOMPLISHING YOUR NEW YEAR'S
RESOLUTION.

H.A.T.E (HAVING ANIMOSITY TOWARDS
EVERYONE) DISEASE.

TOO HAVE SO MUCH HATE, THEY SAY
EVERYTHING STARTS WITH SELF.
SO FOR TO HATE EVERYONE, THAT MEANS YOU
HATE YOURSELF.
IT'S NOT THE WORLD'S FAULT, FOR YOUR
PERSONAL FAILURES AND PROBLEMS.
YOUR NEGATIVE VIBES SO HIGH, YOU NEED TO
TURN DOWN THE VOLUME.
NOBODY WANT TO HEAR THEM, FEEL THEM,
OR SEE THEM.
THE ROOT OF A PROBLEM IS YOU, IT SEEMS TO
WHERE IT ALWAYS STEM.

THEY SAY BIRDS OF A FEATHER FLOCK
TOGETHER, SO IF YOU HAVE A CREW.
TEN TIMES OUT OF TEN, THEY ARE HATERS
LIKE YOU.
FRIENDS AND RELATIONSHIPS DON'T LAST
THAT LONG BEFORE YOU TURN ON EACH
OTHER.
THEY SAY HATE LAST LONGER THAN LOVE, IS
THAT WHY YOU FEEL THAT WAY TOWARDS
ONE ANOTHER.
HATE MOTIVATE, BUT A PERSON DON'T NEED
THAT MUCH MOTIVATION IN THIS WORLD.
SOME PEOPLE STAND TALL THROUGH IT ALL,
SOME CAN'T IT TAKE IT AND CURLED.
THE SAME ENERGY AND THINKING PROCESS
YOU USE, TO TRY TO BRING SOMEONE ELSE
DOWN.
YOU CAN USE TO BETTER YOURSELF, & TO GET
RID OF YOUR MEAN MUG OR FROWN.
I'M NATURALLY VACCINATED BY THE ALL MOST
HIGH, SO YOU CAN NEVER INFECT ME.
ALL YOUR NEGATIVE TALK AND ACTIONS WILL
NEVER EFFECT ME.

TRENDING MINDSET

DO PEOPLE THINK FOR THEMSELVES
NOWADAYS, OR ONLY THINK LIKE WHAT IS
TRENDING.
UNTIL THE MAJORITY AGREE, THE THOUGHTS
IN THEIR MIND BE PENDING.
IF IT ISN'T THE POPULAR OPINION, THEY BE TO

SCARED TO THINK IT OR SAY IT.
ON THE WINNING TEAM AND SAFE SIDE, THEY
ALWAYS WANT TO PLAY WITH.
I WAS RAISED ON A SAYING NO NUTS, NO
GLORY.
ALL THESE CELEBRITY CLONES, WANT TO HAVE
THE SAME STORY.
DO THE SAME THINGS, LIVE THE SAME LIFE.
FIND A BAD B!+<H, TURN HER INTO A WIFE.
COULD KNOW SOMETHING IS DEAD WRONG,
BUT STILL GO ALONG.
LYRICS DUMB AF, THE BEAT GO, BUT SINCE IT'S
THE JAM, THIS IS YOUR SONG.
SINCE MOST BLACK ARE DEMOCRATS, THIS IS
HOW YOU VOTE.
NOT KNOWING OR FOLLOWING WHAT'S
REALLY GOING ON, DON'T TAKE ONE NOTE.
WHEN CONSEQUENCES SETTLE, IT'S EVERYONE
FAULT BUT YOURS.
I KNOW YOU HEARD THE SAYING, WHEN IT
RAINS IT POURS.
DO THE RIGHT THING, THINK FOR YOURSELF
SO YOU WANT HAVE NO REGRETS.
YOU CAN'T RIDE EVERY WAVE, AND BE APART
OF EVERY TREND, FORM YOUR OWN MINDSET.
MORE DEDICATED TO GOING VIRAL, THAN
GETTING RICH.
DIE HARD FAN OF WHAT'S TRENDING, WHEN IT
BECOMES UNPOPULAR YOU SWITCH.
IN MY LUKE SITAL SIGNH VOICE, NOTHING
STAYS THE SAME.
MINDSET STAYS ON WHAT'S TRENDING, DON'T
CARE IF IT'S CORNY OR LAME.

LOVE YOU MOM

I'M THANKFUL FOR YOU & I LOVE YOU MOM,
I READ SCRIPTURES DAILY 6 MONTHS
STRAIGHT, YOU GAVE ME FROM PSALMS.
EACH DAY BRINGS JOY ANEW,
THERE'S NOTHING IN THIS WORLD I WOULDN'T
DO FOR YOU.
YOUR STRONG WILL POWER, AND
UNCONDITIONAL LOVE.
THE ALL MOST HIGH IS ALL I PUT ABOVE.
I'M SO GRATEFUL FOR EVERYTHING YOU DO.
MY GOAL IS TO MAKE YOU HAPPY, AND MAKE
YOUR DREAMS COME TRUE.
YOU GUIDE ME THROUGH LIFE'S CHALLENGES,
WHEN LIFE'S BECOME UNLEVELED, YOU HELP
KEEP BALANCES.
WITH WISDOM PURE AND TRUE,
YOU BRING SUNSHINE, WHEN I'M FEELING SO
BLUE.
I'M THANKFUL FOR YOUR STRENGTH, MOM,
HELPING ME KEEP MY CHAKRAS ALIGNED,
AND KEEPING ME CALM.
FAMILY OVER EVERYTHING, WE STUCK
TOGETHER LIKE GLUE
MY MOTHER'S MY ROCK, & MY GUIDING VIEW.

DETERMINE AFTER DELIBERATION

WRITTEN IN 1996 AS A HIGH SCHOOL
ASSIGNMENT FOR A DANDELION POEM.

I'M STEREOTYPED BECAUSE OF WHAT I AM NOT
WHO I AM.
IF YOU DON'T KNOW ME, TREAT ME LIKE A
BRAND NEW PERSON.
I CAN'T HELP YOUR PAST EXPERIENCE WITH
PEOPLE OF MY KIND.
I REFUSE TO BE PUNISHED FOR SOMEBODY
ELSE'S ACTIONS.
IT TAKES MORE THAN ONE PERSON TO MAKE A
CHANGE.
WE CAN BOTH PLAY HARD AND BE UNWILLING
TO GIVE UP OUR WAYS.
I'LL REFUSE TO FIGHT ALL MY LIFE OR DIE FOR
NOT GETTING RESPECT.
I HAVE BETTER THINGS TO LIVE FOR.
I SEE THE WORLD'S NOT MINE TO CHANGE, ALL
I CAN DO IS FIGHT TO SURVIVE.
MY GOALS ARE TO BE REMEMBERED FOR
ETERNITY; IF NOT I'LL JUST BE SOME ASHES IN
A COFFIN WITH A DECAYING
TOMBSTONE.

MY MINDSET NOW 2022.

I'M STILL STEREOTYPED BECAUSE WHAT I AM
AND WHO I AM.
IF YOU DON'T KNOW ME, YOU SHOULD TAKE
THE TIME TO GET TO KNOW ME.

I WAS BRAINWASHED ON THE PAST
EXPERIENCE OF PEOPLE OF MY KIND.
WE ARE A GREAT PEOPLE, WITH A RICH
HISTORY.
I'M STILL BEING JUDGED BY A BIAS RACIST
PEOPLE.
IT TAKE A NATION OF PEOPLE TO MAKE A
CHANGE.
ALL IT TAKES IS COMMUNICATION AND
UNDERSTANDING, FOR US TO IMPROVE OUR
WAYS.
I BEEN FIGHTING ALL MY LIFE, AND I'LL DIE
FOR MY RESPECT.
I RATHER DIE ON MY FEET, THAN LIVE ON MY
KNEES.
I CAN'T CHANGE THE WORLD BY MYSELF, ALL I
CAN DO IS BE A LIVING EXAMPLE.
MY GOALS ARE TO KEEP POSITIVE ENERGY
ALIVE FOR ETERNITY, AND TRANSCEND TO
THE NEXT DIMENSION.

PHASE VII

REDEMPTION

A SLAVE BY CHOICE

YOU ARE SO CONTEMPT WITH YOUR WAYS AND
YOUR CONDITIONS.
THEY KEEP YOU HOODWINKED SO THEY
CONTINUOUSLY BAMBOOZLE, YOU NEVER
HAVE PREMONITION.
SATISFIED BEING THE BIGGEST CONSUMER, &
STILL GET NO RESPECT.
THEN WANT TO COMPLAIN, BOYCOTT, AND
PROTEST, WHEN YOU FINALLY FEEL THE
NEGLECT.
YOU HAVE THE HIGHEST PERCENTAGE OF
ATHLETES IN THE LEAGUE, BUT NEVER
THOUGHT TO CREATE YOUR OWN.
AFTER ALL THE RACIAL ALLEGATIONS, YOU
STILL FIND AWAY TO GET ALONG.
THEY NEVER SUPPORT YOUR BUSINESSES, LIKE
YOU SUPPORT THEIRS.
THEY LOVE TO EXPLOIT YOUR COMMUNITY,
AND SHOW YOU THEY DON'T CARE
BEEN VOTING DEMOCRATS FOR YEARS, FOR
BROKEN PROMISES AND WELFARE.
YOU GET A LITTLE MONEY AND MOVE TO
THEY COMMUNITY, TO BE NEGLECTED WITH
COLD HEARTED STARES.
DREAMS TO GET OUT THE FIELD AND BECOME
THE HOUSE NEGRO.

RACE BEEN GOING BACKWARDS OR BEING
STAGNATE, NO REAL INSPIRATION TO GROW.
BRAINWASHING YOUR OWN KIND WITH THE
NEGATIVE MINDSETS.
LOOKED AT AMONG OTHER RACES AS SOME
BLIND PETS.
THE ONES THAT GOT THE PEOPLE BEHIND
THEM, BE SCARED TO USE THEY VOICE.
TO COWARDLY TO STAND FOR SOMETHING SO
THEY FALL FOR ANYTHING, TO BE A SLAVE BY
CHOICE.
LOVE REPPING YOUR CITY AND HOOD,
MODERN DAY PLANTATIONS.
HATE BLACK PEOPLE THAT INVEST IN PRISONS,
BUT SUPPORT THE ONES CONTINUOUSLY
DOING SENSELESS CRIME FOR
INCARCERATION.
PAY A LOT OF MONEY TO SUPPORT SOMEONE
ELSE FAMILY NAME BRAND, THEN PROMOTE
THEM FOR FREE.
INSTEAD INVESTING INTO YOUR SELF, SO YOU
CAN BUILD UP YOUR FAMILY TREE.
ABORTION IS ONE OF THE NUMBER REASONS
FOR DEATH IN BLACK NEIGHBORHOODS, THE
RACE IS PRO NO CHOICE.
WE NEED TO FORM OUR OWN AGENDA AND
THINK FOR OURSELVES, AND STOP BEING A
SLAVE BY CHOICE.

SUCCESS IS THE BEST REVENGE

YOU DON'T HAVE TO PROVE NOTHING TO
NOBODY, PROVE IT TO YOURSELF.
ALWAYS TAKE CARE AND PUT THE ALL MOST
HIGH FIRST, YOUR SANITY & HEALTH IS YOUR
WEALTH.
THE WORLD IS NOT FAIR, PEOPLE WILL DO YOU
WRONG.
NEVER GIVE UP ALWAYS REMAIN STRONG.
THE PEOPLE THAT HATE AND ENVY YOU,
KNOW THAT YOU ARE BETTER THAN THEM.
ACTIONS SPEAKS LOUDER THAN WORDS, MOST
TIME THEY WANT CONDEMN.
JUST KEEP DOING WHAT YOUR ARE DOING,
NEVER STOOP TO THEY LEVEL.
KEEP YOUR ENERGY AND SPIRIT POSITIVE AND
HIGH, MAKE IT HARD FOR THE DEVIL.
NEVER LOSE FOCUS, KEEP YOUR EYES ON THE
PRIZE.
ALWAYS BE AWARE, SATAN COMES AS ANYONE
AS A DISGUISE
MOST OF THE TIME IT'S NORMALLY SOMEONE
CLOSE TO YOU, THAT WANT TO SEE YOUR
DOWNFALL.
I ASSUME YOU COMING UP SHORT, MAKE THEM
FEEL TALL.
WHAT DO EXPECT FROM PEOPLE WITH LOW
SELF ESTEEM, THAT DOESN'T LOVE
THEMSELVES.
OTHER PEOPLE TROUBLES AND DOWNFALLS,
MAKE THEM FEEL GOOD ABOUT THEMSELVES.

JUST KEEP GIVING LIFE YOUR BEST, AND YOU
WILL CONTINUE TO AVENGE.
THE END RESULT IS BEING SUCCESSFUL AND
SUCCESS IS THE BEST REVENGE.

SELFISH

IF YOU DON'T TAKE CARE AND LOOK OUT FOR
YOURSELF, WHO WILL.
IT'S A DOG EAT DOG WORLD, MOST PEOPLE
DON'T KEEP IT REAL.
WHEN IT ALL BOILS DOWN, YOUR
ACCOUNTABLE FOR YOUR OWN ACTIONS.
THE MORE YOU BETTER YOURSELF, ON
FRIENDS AND ASSOCIATES YOU'LL HAVE TO
USE SUBTRACTION.
LIFE IS TOO SHORT TO CONTINUE TOO REPEAT
THE SAME LESSON.
IF YOU ARE UNABLE TO DO FOR YOURSELF, TO
WHOM CAN YOU BE A BLESSING.
THE SAME PEOPLE YOU SHOW LOVE AND TAKE
CARE OF, WILL BE IN COMPETITION WITH YOU.
YOU TRY TO BRING THEM UP, BUT DOING
GOOD THEY DON'T WANT TO SEE YOU DO.
DON'T GET ME WRONG, I'M NOT SAYING YOU
SHOULDN'T NEVER DO FOR OTHERS.
WHEN PEOPLE SHOW YOU WHO THEY ARE,
BELIEVE THEIR TRUE COLORS.
YOU CAN'T SAVE OTHERS BEFORE YOURSELF,
THEN EXPECT THEM TOO SAVE YOU.
THEN GET MAD AT THEM, FOR NOT BEING
TRUE.

THE ALL MOST HIGH KNOW YOUR ACTIONS
AND YOUR HEART
CONTINUE TO DO THE RIGHTS THINGS, AND
ALWAYS BE SMART.
IT EASIER TOO ACCEPT CONSEQUENCES FROM
YOUR ACTIONS, AND NOT ACTIONS OF OTHERS.
DEPENDING AND RELYING ON YOURSELF IN
LIFE, WILL GET YOU FURTHER.

I LOVE ME

IF YOU DON'T LOVE YOURSELF, THEN WHO
WILL.
IT'S NOT ABOUT WHAT THEY THINK, IT'S ABOUT
HOW YOU FEEL.
NEVER STOOP TO THEY LEVEL, ALWAYS KEEP
IT REAL.
I KNOW THE DECK IS SET , I STILL PLAY THE
CARDS THAT I'M DEAL.
I'M EIGHT YEARS VEGAN, I KNOW MY HEALTH
IS MY WEALTH.
POSITIVE SOUL AND SPIRIT, HIGH ENERGY AND
VIBES PREPARED FOR MY DEATH.
I HAVE GONE OVER A YEAR WITHOUT BLAZING
NO TREES.
OVER A YEAR WITHOUT DRINKING ALCOHOL,
MY BODY IS PURITY .
I'M OVER A YEAR CELIBATE, I'M WORKING ON
BEING THE BEST ME.
I BEEN BLOCKING OUT THE EVIL SPIRITS AND
NEGATIVE FREQUENCIES.

I FELL DOWN BUT NOW I'M BACK UP.
GET RID OF THE FAKE PEOPLE IN YOUR LIFE, IF
YOU KNOW WHAT'S SUP.
WHEN YOU HIT YOUR NADIR, YOU SEE WHO
REALLY CARE.
TAKE IT ALL AND STRIDE, WE ALL KNOW LIFE
ISN'T FAIR.
I'M LIVING MY LIFE TO THE FULLEST, BEING
ALL I CAN BE.
I CAN LOOK IN THE MIRROR AND SMILE, I LOVE
ME.

ALL FOR THE WORD N!66@

AFTER YEARS OF SLAVERY, MENTAL ABUSE,
TORTURE, AND NO RIGHTS.
STILL TO THIS DAY IT HASN'T ENDED, FOR
EQUALITY WE STILL HAVE TO FIGHT.
THEY BLAME US FOR OUR CONDITIONS, THAT'S
BE FORCE UPON US AS A PEOPLE.
WE NEVER WANTED HANDS OUTS, ALL WE
WANTED TO IS BE TO TREATED EQUAL.
BUT REPARATIONS IS DUE, PLUS
RECONDITIONING AND RECONSTRUCTION.
AFTER YEARS OF RAPE, FORCE LABOR,
SPLITTING FAMILIES, AFTER THE ABDUCTION.
WE HELP BUILD THIS NATION BUT IS TREATED
LIKE AN OUTCAST.
WE SHOULD BE THE RACE WITH HATE, BUT OUR
OPPRESSORS HATE FOREVER LAST.
WE WENT THROUGH ALL THIS MISERY, JUST SO
THEY CAN'T SAY THE WORD NIGGER.

WE USE TO BE KINGS AND QUEENS THEY
CALLED US NEGUS.
WHAT THE PURPOSE OF NOT BEING CALLED A
NIGGER, BUT STILL GET TREATED LIKE ONE.
THEY HATE THAT WE NATURALLY PRODUCE
MELANIN, THAT ABSORB ENERGY FROM THE
SUN.
A NATURAL SUBSTANCE THAT'S WORTH MORE
THAN GOLD.
BLACK DON'T CRACK, IT TAKES A LONG TIME
FOR US TOO LOOK OLD.
WE WERE CREATED IN HIS IMAGE, SO THAT'S
WHY AS A PEOPLE WE HAVE TO REMAIN
BIGGER.
PEOPLE GIVE WORDS POWER, I KNOW WHO I
AM, AND IT'S NOT A NIGGER.

I USED TO LOVE H.E.R.

SHE WAS MY ALL, I COULDN'T IMAGINE LIFE
WITHOUT H.E.R.
SHE HELP ME TO SEE THINGS CLEARLY, WHEN
LIFE WAS SUCH A BLUR.
FOR EVERY FEELING AND EMOTION, SHE HAD
SOME WORDS THAT SOOTHE MY SOUL.
WITH H.E.R IN MY LIFE, I ALWAYS FELT WHOLE.
MAYBE I OUT GREW HER, OR SHE JUST BECAME
IMMATURE.
H.E.R MELODIES USE TO TOUCH MY SOUL, H.E.R.
MESSAGE WAS PURE.
NOW SHE ALL ABOUT MATERIALISTIC ITEMS,
DRUGS AND KILLING.

BLOWING THE MOST MONEY, AND TALKING
ABOUT DRUG DEALING.
NOT THINKING OF THE YOUTH SHE
INFLUENCE, THAT LOVE AND LOOK UP TO
H.E.R.
THE WAY SHE MADE THINGS NOW, COMPARED
TO HOW THEY ONCE WERE.
WE USE TO BLAME IT ON THE SYSTEM, BUT
NOW WE HAVE MORE CONTROL.
WE ARE OUR BIGGEST ENEMY NOW, SHE
LIVING LIFE WITH NO SOUL.
AS LONG AS YOU ARE RIDING FOREIGN,
WEARING DESIGNER, AND HAVE A BANK ROLL.
SHE WILL LOVE AND ACCEPT YOU, NOT CARING
ABOUT THE INCARCERATION OR DEATH TOLL.
SHE ONLY LIKE THE YOUNG FELLAS, THE O.G'S
ARE NO LONGER COOL.
SHE ISN'T LOOKING FOR NO ONE TO TEACH
HER BETTER, IF SO SHE WOULD OF STAYED IN
SCHOOL.
NEVER IN THIS LIFETIME, I'D NEVER THOUGHT
THESE FEELINGS WOULD OCCUR.
AT ONE POINT SHE WAS MY ALL, I USE TO LOVE
H.E.R.

THIS IS WHAT IT COME TOO.

THESE DUDES GOSSIP AND D!<K RIDE MORE
THEN THE FEMALES THESE DAYS.
ALWAYS TALKING ABOUT WHAT THE NEXT
MAN GOT, INSTEAD OF MAKING YOUR OWN
WAYS.

ALWAYS TRYING TO BE ON THE SCENE TO
TAKE PICTURES WITH CELEBS, A MALE
GROUPIE.
TRYING TO STAY HIP TO THE TRENDS, EVEN IF
IT MAKE YOU LOOK GOOFY.
WILL SAY AND DO ANYTHING JUST TO GO
VIRAL.
SUPPOSED TO BE GANGSTER, BUT A FEMALE IS
YOUR BIGGEST RIVAL.
GO ALONG WITH ANYTHING, EVEN IF YOU
KNOW IT'S FLAW.
STAND FOR SOMETHING OR FALL FOR
ANYTHING, THAT'S LAW.
I GUESS IT'S HARD TOO FAULT YOU, YOU JUST
FOLLOWING YOUR IDOL THAT'S LAME.
WHEN THE TRUTH GET EXPOSED, THEY NEVER
FEEL SHAME.
THEY JUST MAKE AN EXCUSE AND MOVE ON TO
THE NEXT.
SEE THEM FACE TO FACE AND SAY NOTHING,
BUT HAVE SO MUCH TO SAY IN A TEXT.
OR THEY JUST TWEET, POST, COMMENT OR
INBOX.
BE TRYING TO ACT SO HOOD, BUT NEVER BEEN
ON NO BLOCK.
THEN WHEN THE CONSEQUENCE KICK IN,
THEY WANT TO ACT CIVIL.
THESE NEW ERA DUDES AREN'T STRAIGHT UP,
THEY ARE SWIVEL.
REAL MEN ARE BECOMING RARE THESE DAYS,
YOU LUCKY TO FIND ONE OUT A FEW.
MEN WITH FEMININE WAYS, THIS IS WHAT IT
COME TOO.

HIGHER POWER

WE ALL KNOW IT'S A HIGHER POWER, THAT'S
BIGGER THAN US.
IT'S A SENSITIVE TOPIC, WITH LOWER
INTELLIGENCE QUOTIENT PEOPLE YOU CAN'T
DISCUSS.
MAN PUT THE ALL MOST HIGH IN THE IMAGE
AND CHARACTERISTICS OF A MAN, AND CALL
THEM GOD.
TO CONVERT YOUR SPIRITUALITY INTO
RELIGION, IT'S ALL A FAÇADE.
THE ALL MOST HIGH CAN DIRECTLY GET AT
YOU, THE ALL HAS NO REASON TO TALK TO
YOU
THROUGH NO ONE ELSE.
MOST PEOPLE ARE VICTIMS OF THE WORLD,
WITH POOR SPIRITUAL AND MENTAL HEALTH.
LIVING TO IMPRESS MAN, INSTEAD OF THE ALL
MOST HIGH.
MAJORITY ARE SLOW TO LISTEN, BUT QUICK TO
REPLY.
MISLED TO THINK THEY CAN SIN ALL THEY
LIFE, ASK FORGIVENESS THEN LIVE IN THE SKY.
EVERYONE WANT TO GO TO HEAVEN, BUT
NOBODY WANTS TO DIE.
SOULFUL PEOPLE ARE NATURAL, THE
BRAINWASHED IS MAN-MADE.
FOLLOW YOUR OWN INTUITION, WASTED TIME
CAN'T BE REPAID.
HOW CAN A MAN TELL YOU YOUR DESTINY,
NOT KNOWING HIS OWN.

YOU SUPPOSE TO PUT AWAY YOUR CHILDISH
WAYS OF THINKING, SPEAKING, AND
REASONING, ONCE YOU GET GROWN.
SOME THINGS ARE BEYOND YOUR
UNDERSTANDING, BUT IF YOU SEEK YOU
SHALL FIND.
OPEN YOUR EYES AND FIND YOUR WAY, DON'T
FOLLOW THE BLIND LEADING THE BLIND.
KEEP YOUR SPIRITS AND ENERGY POSITIVE
AND HIGH, BECAUSE SATAN IS ALWAYS TRYING
TO DEVOUR.
KEEP YOUR FAITH IN KNOWING THAT THERE IS
A HIGHER POWER.

THE GOOD, THE BAD, THE COMPLICATED LOVE

LOVE CAN BE THE GREATEST FEELING IN LIFE,
ESPECIALLY WHEN IT'S DISTRIBUTED BACK AT
THE SAME LEVEL.
LOVE CAN ALSO BE A HURTING FEELING,
WHEN YOUR DECEIVED BY A DEVIL.
THE HEART IS DECEITFUL ABOVE ALL THINGS,
AND DESPERATELY WICKED: WHO CAN KNOW
IT?
MOST PEOPLE TRUE FEELINGS, THEY NEVER
EXPRESS IT OR SHOW IT.
LOVE IS VERY COMPLEX, DEPENDING ON YOUR
RELATIONSHIP WITH THE INDIVIDUAL.
GOD IS LOVE, THE BASIC INSTRUCTIONS
BEFORE LEAVING EARTH ARE BIBLICAL.
THE AVERAGE HUMAN IS CAUGHT UP IN
WORLDLY WAYS, ONLY WORRIED ABOUT THEIR
OWN WELL BEING.

BEING IN THE NEXT PERSON SHOES, OR THE
BIGGER PICTURE THEY ARE NEVER SEEING.
THE ACTIONS DISPLAYED WHEN THINGS DON'T
GO THEY WAY, OR THEY DON'T GET WHAT
THEY WANT.
THE THINGS IN LIFE THEY WANT BUT CAN'T
HAVE, THEY CONTINUOUSLY TAUNT.
HAVING TRUE LOVE, YOU NEVER WANT LIFE
TO END.
IMAGINE LIVING IN HARMONY WITH EVERY
ONE BEING LIKE FAMILY AND FRIENDS.
THE PEOPLE YOU LOVE THE MOST, SEEMS TO
BE THE ONES THAT MOSTLY HURT YOU.
SATAN COMES IN ALL FORMS AND FASHION,
NEVER LET IT DIVERT YOU.
A SMOOTH SEA NEVER MADE A SKILLED
SAILOR.
LIVE LIFE ON HIGH AND POSITIVE
FREQUENCIES, NEVER BECOME A WAILER.
LIFE HAS MANY DIFFERENT PHASES, SO BELOW
AS ABOVE.
THE GOOD, THE BAD, THE COMPLICATED
LOVE.
WORKING OUT DIFFICULT TIMES, ONLY MAKE
THE LOVE MORE REAL.
IT'S SMARTER TO REACT OFF THINKING,
INSTEAD OF HOW YOU FEEL.

VIRAL

THEY USE TO SAY THE LOVE OF MONEY IS THE
ROOT OF ALL EVIL, NOWADAYS IT'S
ATTENTION.
THE THINGS PEOPLE WILL DO FOR A LIKE,
FOLLOW, COMMENT, OR MENTION.
VOLUNTARILY DISGRACE THEMSELVES, FOR 5
MINUTES OF FAME.
THE REPERCUSSIONS IS A LIFETIME FULL OF
SHAME.
NO EXCUSES, BLAMING IT ON BEING YOUNG
AND WILD.
NOWADAYS, IT'S MORE OF THE ADULTS THEN
THE CHILD.
THE TONGUE HAS THE POWER OF LIFE AND
DEATH, AND THOSE WHO LOVE IT WILL EAT
IT'S FRUIT.
THE ONE SPEAKING RECKLESSLY JUST FOR
ATTENTION, NEVER THINK ABOUT THE MINDS
THEY
POLLUTE.
SOME PEOPLE DONE LOST THEY LIFE, TRYING
TO PULL A FOOLISH STUNT.
ALL ATTENTION ISN'T GOOD, IS IT REALLY
WORTH IT, IS THIS IS WHAT YOU REALLY WANT.
SOME DISPLAY THEMSELVES TO THE WORLD
FOR FREE.
THEN COMPLAIN WHY THEY CAN'T FIND
NOBODY.
ALWAYS REPEATING WHAT'S TRENDING OR
LOOKING FOR A CHALLENGE.
IT'S LIKE ALL YOUR BRAIN CELLS ARE DEAD, SO
ONLINE FOR THOUGHTS YOU HAVE TO

SCAVENGE.
AS QUICKLY UP, TEN TIMES FASTER DOWN
YOUR LIFE WILL SPIRAL.
FROM ACTING OUT OF CHARACTER JUST TO GO
VIRAL.

TROLLS

SOCIAL MEDIA IS A COWARD DREAM COME
TRUE.
TOO COMMENT THINGS, FACE TO FACE THEY
KNOW THEY WOULDN'T SAY TO YOU.
I'M SURE THEY TALK CRAZY JUST TO GET
ATTENTION.
HOPING TO GET A REPLY OR A MENTION.
HIDING BEHIND AN ALIAS NAME, WITH A FAKE
PICTURE
IN PUBLIC THEY ARE A REJECT, NEVER BEEN
PART OF THE MIXTURE.
BE CAREFUL NOT TO FALL VICTIM OR GET
CAUGHT UP IN THEY TRAP.
THEY DON'T EVEN MEAN WHAT THEY SAY, ALL
THEY DO IS CAP.
"NEVER ARGUE WITH A FOOL; ONLOOKERS
MAY NOT BE ABLE TO TELL THE DIFFERENCE."
THE TROLL ALREADY WINS, WHEN HE HAVE
YOU BECOME BELLIGERENCE.
WHO'D EVER THINK WE WOULD SEE THE
WORLD COME TO THIS
PEOPLE THAT HAVEN'T EVER ACCOMPLISHED
NOTHING, BUT ALWAYS CRITICIZE AND DISS.
THE SAD THING ABOUT THAT, PEOPLE MAKE A
CAREER OUT OF DOING SO.

PUTTING THEY TWO SENSE IN TO THINGS THEY
DON'T KNOW.
IT ALWAYS LOOK DIFFERENT FROM THE
OUTSIDE LOOKING IN.
NOWADAYS POINTING OUT REASONABLE
DOUBTS, AND HAVING COMMON SENSE IS A
SIN.
WHEN I SEE THIRST TRAPS A IGNORANT POST I
CONTINUE TO SCROLL.
TIME IS OF THE ESSENCE, WHY WASTE IT ON A
TROLL

THE HATE IS REAL

THE TIME YOU SPEND PLOTTING ON
DESTROYING ME, YOU CAN SPEND ON
BETTERING YOURSELF.
TO HAVE SO MUCH HATE FOR SOMEBODY, YOU
HAVE TO HATE THYSELF.
YOU HAVE THE MIND OF AN OXYMORON, YOU
DON'T WANT BUT WANT FROM ME.
YOU LIKE THE DAUGHTER OF SANFORD SON,
YOU LIL BIG DUMMY.
IT'S SEEMS LIKE YOU OBSESSED, WITH LOVING
TO HATE ME.
I SEE THE DEVIL BEEN BUSY USING YOU
LATELY.
YOU AREN'T WORTH MY ENERGY OR MY TIME.
I'M SO ENLIGHTEN, YOU DON'T HAVE TO TRY
TO STEAL, I'LL GIVE YOU SOME SHINE.

WHEN IT'S ALL OVER WITH, WILL IT REALLY BE
WORTH IT.
THE SECRET IS IT'S THE ALL PLAN, YOU'LL
NEVER UNEARTH THIS.
ONLY A FOOL FOCUS ON WHAT'S DOWN, YOU
FOCUS ON WHAT'S UP.
THE WISE MOVE IN SILENCE, THAT'S WHY I
SHUT UP.
YOU AREN'T WORTH MY ATTENTION, BUT I
HEAR YOU AND I SEE YOU.
I JUST PUT IN THE MOST HIGH HANDS, SHE'LL
GUARANTEE YOU.
IRON SHARPEN IRON, STEEL SHARPEN STEEL.
I CAN TRULY SEE THE HATE IS REAL.

THE LOVE IS FAKE

YOU NEVER HEAR FROM THEM UNTIL THEY
NEED SOMETHING.
IT'S ALWAYS ANOTHER, IT'S NEVER JUST THE
ONE THING.
THE ONE OUT OF ONE HUNDRED TIMES, YOU
TURN THEM DOWN, YOU ARE EVERYTHING BUT
A CHILD OF GOD.
AT ONE POINT YOU THOUGHT IT WAS REAL
LOVE, IT'S ALWAYS BEEN FRAUD.
THESE DAYS YOU HAVE TO DIE TO RECEIVE
YOUR FLOWERS.
ALL THE TIME YOU PUT IN TRYING TO FORM A
GENUINE RELATIONSHIP WAS WASTED HOURS.
IF ONLY WHEN YOUR ALIVE, YOU COULD
RECEIVE TEN PERCENT OF THE LOVE THEY

HAVE FOR YOU WHEN YOUR DIE.
YOU COULD HAVE BEEN LIVING LIFE ON A
NATURAL HIGH.
THE HATE BE SO REAL, THE LOVE BE SO FAKE.
HOW MUCH EFFORT IN BEING REAL DOES IT
REALLY TAKE.
THE ONES THAT SO CALL LOVE YOU, BE THE
REASON OF YOUR DEATH.
THEN THEY SAY WHAT THEY WOULD OF,
COULD OF, AND SHOULD OF DID, WHEN YOU
NO LONGER HAVE BREATH.
WHILE YOU ARE ALIVE, YOUR ONLY GOOD AS
YOUR LAST CHARITABLE ACT.
THE TRUTH HURTS, SO THEY HATE TO HEAR
THE FACTS.
AS LONG AS IT MAKE THEM FEEL GOOD, THEY
RATHER LIVE A LIE.
TO THINK ABOUT IT, THE FAKE LOVE
CONTINUES, EVEN AFTER YOU DIE.
BUT THEY ARE SPIRITUAL AND SAY GOD IS
LOVE.
THEY ARE JUST WASTED ENERGY, IN THIS
WORLD THEY ARE CONFORMED OF.

KNOW IT ALL

NOWADAYS THEY KNOW IT ALL, UNTIL THEY
ARE PUT IN THE SITUATION.
THE FIRST LINK THEY SEE AFTER THEY
GOOGLE, IS WHERE THEY GET THEIR
INFORMATION.

IT'S A WELL-KNOWN FACT, THAT EXPERIENCE
IS THE BEST TEACHER.
BUT THEY IGNORE THE EXPERIENCE PERSON,
SAYING THEY SOUND LIKE A PREACHER.
LEARNING FROM YOUR ELDER, IS LIFE CHEAT
CODE.
WHY KEEP REPEATING THE SAME ACTIONS,
ENDING UP IN THE SAME MODE.
YOU CAN'T TELL THEM NOTHING, THEY HAVE
IT ALL FIGURED OUT.
MOST FAIL THINKING THEY BETTER THAN
YOU, AND THAT'S EVEN WITH A EASIER ROUTE.
A WISE PERSON NEVER KNOWS IT ALL, ONLY
FOOL KNOWS EVERYTHING.
AND THINKING YOU KNOW IT ALL, COULD BE A
DANGEROUS AND DEADLY THING.
YOU STOP THINKING, WHEN YOU THINK
THERE'S NOTHING ELSE TO LEARN.
DO YOUR THOUGHTS ONLY BENEFIT YOU, OR
DO YOU THINK FOR OTHER PEOPLE
CONCERNS.
THE SMALLER YOUR REALITY, THE MORE
CONVINCED OF YOUR ALL KNOWING.
WHEN YOU STOP WATERING SEEDS, THEY STOP
GROWING.
ALWAYS BE WILLING TO SEEK, LISTEN, AND
LEARN, TO EXPAND YOUR KNOWLEDGE.
SO YOU CAN BE ENLIGHTEN, LIVING WITH
HIGH WATTAGE.

SLAVERY IS A CHOICE

THEY SO USE TO HAVING CHAINS AROUND
THEY NECK, NOW THEY BUY OVERPRICED
ONES AND PUT THEM AROUND
THEY NECK THEMSELVES.
THEY SO USE TO BEING MISTREATED, NOW
THEY TURN AGAINST EACH OTHER AND KILL
THEMSELVES.
THEY USE TO GET KILLED FROM FOR
KNOWING HOW READ, BUT NOW WANT PICK UP
A BOOK AND LEARN FOR THEMSELVES
SO USE TO BEING BRANDED, NOW THEY OVER
PAY AND ADVERTISE FOR FREE, TO BRAND
THEMSELVES.
EVEN IF THE BRAND OWNER DOESN'T LIKE
THEM, AND FEEL LIKE THE MASTER OF THE
SLAVES.
THEY COME FROM KINGS AND QUEENS, NOW
THEY ACT LIKE THEY COME FROM THE CAVES.
REPRESENTING A STATE, CITY, PROJECT, AND
STREET, WHERE THEY ANCESTORS DIDN'T
CONQUER BUT WERE FORCED TO
LIVE.
AND WILLING TO DIE FOR THE RESPECT OF IT,
THE ONLY THING THEY LEAVE THEY LOVE
ONES TO GIVE.
KNOW OTHER RACES ARE RACIST AGAINST
THEM, BUT THEY ARE IN A RACE WITH
THEMSELVES.
THEY QUICK TO CLAIM AND TAKE UP FOR
ANOTHER RACE, AND LOVE TO HATE AND
TURN ON THEMSELVES.

SLAVERY WAS A CHOICE, DO YOUR RESEARCH
ON THE NATIVE AMERICANS.
THEY WERE IN TUNED WITH NATURE, NOT
WAITING ON A MESSIAH TO COME.
NOW SLAVERY IS A CHOICE, IT'S MORE MENTAL
NOW.
WHY WOULD YOUR OPPRESSOR WANT YOU TO
BE FREE, AND SHOW YOU HOW.
THE ONLY RACE THAT ARE WILLINGLY DOING
THINGS, OTHER RACES WANT DO.
THEN WHEN THE CONSEQUENCES OF THE
ACTIONS KICK IN, BLAME EVERYONE BUT YOU.
BECOME LEADERS FOR THEIR MATERIALISTIC,
AND OPPRESSOR GIVING STATUS, AND NOT
THEY ACTIONS AND VOICE.
CONTINUING THE SAME ACTIVITIES IN
DIFFERENT FASHIONS, SLAVERY IS YOUR
CHOICE.

F.E.A R. (FACE EVERYTHING AND RISE)

IT WAS WRITTEN, THE MOST HIGH WOULDN'T
PUT MORE ON YOU THAN YOU CAN BEAR.
THE MORE TRIALS YOU ENDURE, MAKE YOU
HARDER TO COMPARE.
NO LIFE IS PERFECT, YOU GOT TO TAKE THE
GOOD WITH THE BAD.
UNTIL IT'S GONE, YOU NEVER KNOW WHAT
YOU HAD.
THEY SAY IT'S BETTER TO BE FEARED THAN
LOVED.

I RATHER BE REALLY HATED, THAN FALSELY
LOVED.
I COULD NEVER FORGET EVERYTHING AND
RUN, I'LL ALWAYS FACE EVERYTHING AND RISE.
IT'LL ONLY MAKE ME STRONGER, IF IT ISN'T
THE CAUSE OF MY DEMISE.
THE FEARS YOU DON'T FACE, WILL BECOME
YOUR LIMITS.
YOU CAN'T LIVE YOUR LIFE TO THE FULLEST, IF
YOUR ARE ALWAYS TIMID.
SO THINGS ARE EASIER SAID THAN DONE, LIKE
LIVE LIFE WITH NO FEAR.
UNTIL YOU ARE PUT IN THAT POSITION, YOU'LL
NEVER KNOW HOW YOU'D REACT UNTIL YOU
ARE THERE.
REMEMBER WHAT DON'T KILL YOU, ONLY
MAKE YOU STRONG.
BELIEVE IN THE HIGHER POWER, AND YOU
WILL ALWAYS LIVE ON.
EVEN IF YOU FAIL, ALWAYS GIVE IT MORE
TRIES.
NEVER BE AFRAID, FACE EVERYTHING AND
RISE.

HYPE

TOO BE ACCEPTED, THEY JUST GO ALONG
WITH THE FLOW.
THEY DON'T CARE WHAT DIRECTION IT'S
TAKING THEM, ALONG WITH EVERYONE ELSE
THEY JUST WANT TO GO.

SAYING WHAT THEY HEARD OR READ, NOT
GIVING IT NO THOUGHT.
TOO FEEBLE MINDED TOO KNOW IT'S B.S, THAT
THEY JUST BROUGHT.
PEOPLE WILL GO FOR ANYTHING THEY DON'T
UNDERSTAND, IF IT GOT ENOUGH HYPE.
NO ORIGINAL IDEAS, ONLY TRENDING TOPICS
THEY TYPE.
ONE DAY IT'S HERE, NEXT DAY IT'S GONE.
NEVER TO BE MENTIONED AGAIN, OR
THOUGHT ABOUT TO BE SPOKEN ON.
THE WORLD IS FILLED WITH MINIONS.
WITH NOTHING BUT REGURGITATED
OPINIONS.
THEY LOVE REACTING TO IGNORANT AND
NEGATIVE SPOOFS.
BUT THEY BE SO HURT AND OFFENDED, WHEN
THEY HEAR THE TRUTH.
"DON'T BELIEVE THE HYPE", IS SOMETHING
PUBLIC ENEMY BEEN SAID.
CAUGHT UP IN THE HYPE, HAVE SO MANY
PEOPLE MISLED.
THE PEOPLE ARE THE SHEEP, SOCIAL MEDIA
TRENDING TOPICS ARE THEY SHEPHERD.
OPEN YOUR THIRD EYE AND MEDITATE FIRST,
BEFORE YOU GO WITH WHAT YOU HEARD.

YOU CAN'T PLEASE EVERYBODY

YOU CAN'T PLEASE EVERYONE, SO IT'S BEST TO
DO WHAT MAKE YOU HAPPY.
WHEN YOU DO SOMETHING TO PLEASE
SOMEONE, BUT THEY SHOW YOU THEY DON'T
CARE IN RETURN, THAT FEELING'S
CRAPPIE.
SO IT'S BEST TO DO WHAT'S IN YOUR BEST
INTEREST.
OR YOU WOULD END UP PAYING FOR IT WITH
INTEREST.
IF THEY ARE TRULY DOWN FOR YOU, THEY'D
STICK WITH YOU THROUGH NO MATTER WHAT.
AND YOU WOULDN'T HAVE TO WORRY ABOUT
NO IF, AND, OR BUT.
I DON'T KNOW THE KEY TO SUCCESS, BUT THE
KEY TO FAILURE IS TRYING TO PLEASE
EVERYBODY.
THE ALL MOST HIGH KNOW YOUR HEART, NO
MATTER WHATEVER, GOD SEE.
MOST PEOPLE ARE SEASONAL ANYWAY, JUST
PROPS ON YOUR JOURNEY.
MOST WANT COME TO YOUR DEFENSE, UNLESS
IT'S BENEFITING THEM LIKE AN ATTORNEY.
IF YOU MANAGE TO PLEASE EVERYONE, BEST
BELIEVE THERE'S SOMETHING WRONG.
IT WILL ONLY BE FOR A SHORT WHILE, BUT THE
REPERCUSSIONS WILL BE VERY LONG.
THEY LOVE YOU, TO HATE YOU, TO LOVE YOU
AGAIN.
THAT'S WHY YOU GOT TO DO WHAT MAKES
YOU HAPPY, YOUR LEGACY IS ALL YOU HAVE IN
THE END.

LIFE'S LIKE A RUBIK'S CUBE, IT'S HARD TO GET
ALL SIDES TO COORDINATE.
DON'T MAKE TRYING TO MAKE EVERYONE
HAPPY, DETERMINE YOUR FATE.

STAY ALERT

NO MATTER
HOW HARD YOU TRY
TOO DO WELL.
EVIL SPIRITS
WOULD LOVE TOO SEE
YOU FAIL.

EUREKA

I AM GREAT
I LOVE ME
I AM AWESOME
LIFE'S A BLESSING
IN DISGUISE

WRITERS BLOCK

UNMOTIVATED, BOTHERED, AND UNINSPIRED.
SEEKING ON OBTAINING ALL THE THINGS
THAT I DESIRE.
ON LIFE'S TREADMILL CHASING AFTER THE ALL
MIGHTY DOLLAR.
SOME SITUATIONS IN LIFE MAKE YOU WANT TO
HOLLER.
WE SHOULD BE IMMUNE TO THE EMOTIONS,
BECAUSE THE ACTIONS CONSTANTLY REPEAT.
DEPENDING ON A SUBSTANCE, SO YOU CAN
MENTALLY RETREAT.
THEY CAN'T HANDLE THE TRUTH, SO YOU
HAVE TO BE DISCREET.
BECOME INTROVERTED AND LIVE VERY
DISCRETE.
TRYING TO AVOID THE NEGATIVE ENERGY,
LOW FREQUENCIES AND BAD VIBES.
FEELING LIKE A LOST SOUL CAST AWAY FROM
MY TRIBE.
TRYING TO CONTROL WHAT WAS DESTINE TO
BE.
IT'S ALL A FAÇADE, THE THINGS THEY DON'T
WANT YOU TOO SEE.
BUT YOU'D SWEAR THEY WERE MAGICIANS
BECAUSE IT'S RIGHT IN YOUR FACE.
UNDERSTANDING MATTER, ENERGY, TIME AND
SPACE.
I HAD TO MEDITATE, SO MY THOUGHTS I
COULD UNLOCK.
NOW I'M BACK FOCUSED, SNAPPED OUT THIS
WRITER'S BLOCK

PROUD OF ME

WAKE UP EVERYDAY, IT'S JUST ANOTHER DAY
ANOTHER DOLLAR.
BUT ON YOUR DEATH BED, IT'S ALL ABOUT
ANOTHER DAY, NOT A DOLLAR.
LIFE, WE ARE ALL TRYING TO FIGURE IT OUT,
AS WE GO.
SOCIETY CAPITALIZE OFF OF THE THINGS WE
DON'T KNOW.
CONSTANTLY LEARNING FROM OUR MISTAKES
AS WE GO.
TRYING TO AVOID THE FALL, WHILE GOING
ALONG WITH THE FLOW.
TRYING TO LIVE GOOD, AND AVOID LIVING
POOR.
SOON AS WE OBTAIN GOOD, WE THRIVE FOR
MORE.
IT'S NEVER TO MUCH, AND IT'S NEVER
ENOUGH.
THE THINGS THAT YOU WILL SETTLE FOR,
WHEN THE GOING GET TOUGH.
YOU'LL NEVER KNOW WHAT YOU'LL DO, UNTIL
YOU ARE PUT IN THAT POSITION.
IT MIGHT NOT AFFECT YOU NOW, BUT DOWN
THE LINE YOU'LL PAY FOR YOUR DECISION.
TRYING TO BECOME A GOAT, CHASING LEGAL
TENDER NOTES.
WHILE AVOIDING A BACK STAB, OR A CUT TO
THE THROAT.
I'LL JUST PLAY THE CARD'S I WAS DEALT, BEING
THE BEST I CAN BE.
SO WHEN IT'S ALL OVER, THE MOST HIGH WILL
BE PROUD OF ME.

LIFE'S IMPATIENT

TIME DON'T WAIT FOR NO MAN, YOU GOT TO
KEEP ON MOVING.
SEEMS LIKE THEY'LL NEVER KNOW, SO YOU
GOT TO KEEP PROVING.
IF YOU KNOW THYSELF, YOU'D CARELESS
ABOUT WHAT THEY THINK.
DON'T GET CAUGHT UP IN THE MUD, OR THE
QUICK SAND AND SLOWLY SINK.
YOU WAS JUST YOUNG, NOW YOUR OLD, IT
HAPPENS IN THE QUICK OF A BLINK.
MOST PEOPLE LOSE THEMSELVES TRYING TO
STAY IN SYNC.
FIGHTING WITH FATHER TIME, TRYING TO
REMAIN FOREVER YOUNG.
HATING ON THE YOUTH, BUT TRYING TO
REMAIN FOREVER YOUNG.
LIFE'S LIKE SCHOOL, IT'S ABOUT GRADUATING
TO THE NEXT LEVEL.
PROPERLY USE YOUR GOD GIVEN GIFTS, DON'T
GET USED BY THE DEVIL.
DON'T BE A WOULD OF, COULD OF, SHOULD OF,
USE YOUR TIME WISELY.
LIFE WILL PASS YOU BY, STAYING HIGH AS YOU
CAN BE.
FATHER TIME IS UNDEFEATED, SO LIVE YOUR
LIFE TO THE FULLEST.
ALWAYS GIVE IT YOUR ALL, NEVER SETTLE FOR
LESS.
DON'T NEVER GET TOO CONTEMPT, BECAUSE
THERE'S ALWAYS A REPLACEMENT.
TAKE YOUR TIME DO IT RIGHT, BECAUSE LIFE'S
IMPATIENT.

PHASE VIII

THE VISION

TRANSCEND

I'M TRYING TO FULFILL MY DESTINY, BEFORE
MY TIME EXPIRES.
I'M BECOMING LESS INSPIRED, I'M STARTING TO
LOSE MY FIRE.
THINGS ARE BECOMING LESS INTERESTED,
THAT I USE TO DESIRE.
FEELING LIKE THIS, I KNOW IT'S TIME FOR ME
TO RETIRE.
I CAN'T REST IN PEACE, UNTIL I MAKE MY
FAMILY PROUD.
I ALWAYS WENT AGAINST THE GRAIN, I NEVER
ROLLED WITH THE CROWD.
LOSING SO MANY FAMILY AND FRIENDS, I HAVE
A DIFFERENT PERSPECTIVE ON LIFE.
WILL I GO OUT LIKE JESUS, AND NEVER HAVE A
WIFE.
THIS IS AN AWESOME DIMENSION, JUST TO
MUCH NEGATIVE ENERGY.
I TRIED TO NOT CONFORM TO THIS WORLD,
AND BE THE BEST ME.
BURY MY REMAINS WITH SEEDS, SO I CAN
BECOME A TREE OF LIFE.
AS LONG AS I KNOW I GAVE IT MY ALL, TO LIVE
MY BEST LIFE.
STAY IN TUNE WITH NATURE, STAYING
ALIGNED WITH THE STARS.
I DWELL ON EARTH, BUT MY MIND ON MARS.

I ALWAYS REMAIN SOLID, I'LL NEVER BEND.
I PRAY THAT I FULFILL MY DESTINY, BEFORE I
TRANSCEND.

THIRD EYE ACTIVE

AS THE SUN BEAM DOWN ON MY PINEAL
GLAND, I AM FULLY WOKE.
I RID MY LIFE OF ALL NEGATIVE THINGS,
BEFORE MY SPIRIT BROKE.
I KEEP MY CHAKRAS ALIGNED, REST TO KEEP
MY BODY HEALING.
IT'S BEST TO GO WITH YOUR THOUGHTS,
INSTEAD OF HOW YOU FEELING.
SEEING THROUGH THE VICIOUS RUMORS, AND
DANGEROUS LIES.
THEY'LL TELL IT TO YOU STRAIGHT, LOOKING
YOU IN THE EYES.
THEY TELL IT TO YOU THROUGH THEIR
PERSPECTIVE, SO IT'S HIS STORY.
IF YOU WASN'T THERE, YOU'LL NEVER GET THE
TRUE HISTORY.
FOOL ME ONCE SHAME ON YOU, FOOL ME
TWICE SHAME ON ME.
DO YOUR OWN RESEARCH, EDUCATE YOURSELF
TO BE.
FULLY MELANATED, I'M CONNECTED TO THE
SUN.
I'M A PRODUCT OF THE ALL MOST HIGH, IT'S
NOTHING I DONE.
6 PROTONS, 6 NEUTRONS, 6 ELECTRONS, WITH 6
SENSE.

I'M BUILT TO CARRY ON, EVEN WHEN IT GET
TOO TENSE.
I LEARNED TO BE STRAIGHT FORWARD, AND
NOT TO BE RETRACTIVE.
AND STAY FULLY AWARE AND KEEP MY THIRD
EYE ACTIVE

FREE SPIRIT

I AM A SPIRITUAL BEING, I AM NOT RELIGIOUS.
I'M AN ORIGINAL MAN, MY ANCESTORS ARE
INDIGENOUS.
I'M BEING LEAD BY MY SPIRIT, I'M NOT
CONFORMING TO THIS WORLD.
A PRODUCT OF NATURE, AS IF I WAS A
DIAMOND OR A PEARL.
I'M LEAD BY THE SPIRIT OF GOD, NOT MAN
WAYS.
BECAUSE MAN CHANGES LIKE THE WEATHER
OF THE DAYS.
NOT KNOWING HIS OWN DESTINY, BUT TRY TO
LEAD THE MASS.
IN GOD HE TRUST, BUT HE WILL DO ANYTHING
FOR CASH.
THEY SAY THE LORD KNOWS OUR LIFE FROM A
TO Z.
BUT IF WE FALL SHORT, HOW ARE WE HELD
FOR ACCOUNTABILITY.
TOO MANY CONTRADICTIONS, I THINK IT'S ALL
MAN IDEA'S.
90% OF THE WORLD BEING SHEEPLE, IS HOW
THEY WANT TO SEE US.

MY SOUL IS FROM ELSEWHERE, I'M SURE OF
THAT, AND I INTEND TO END UP THERE.
IN THIS REALM WE ARE UNEQUALLY JUDGE,
WITH THEM KNOWING LIFE ISN'T FAIR.
LET YOUR MIND SET YOU FREE FROM CONTROL
OF OTHER INFLUENCE.
I WILL FOREVER KEEP MY FREEDOM AND
POSITIVE SPIRIT IN CONFLUENCE.

MADE IN AMERICA

SNATCHED FROM OUR HOMELAND, THEY
ERASED OUR HISTORY.
TRUE KNOWLEDGE OF OUR ANCESTORS IS A
MYSTERY.
EVEN THOUGH THERE'S PROOF, WE WERE
HERE BEFORE THEY CAME.
400 PLUS YEARS OF SLAVERY, BUT WE ARE THE
BLAME.
FOR ALL THEM YEARS OF THE CONDITIONING
AND PROGRAMMING.
WE WERE FORCED TO PRAY TO THEY GOD, FOR
THE JAM WE ARE IN.
WE USE TO GET SOLD OR KILLED FOR
KNOWING HOW TO READ OR WRITE, NOW
THEY SAY WE ARE DUMB.
WE GOT A LONG WAY TO GO, BUT LOOK HOW
FAR WE HAVE COME.
MURDERED, RAPED, AND TORTURED,
GENERATIONS OF P.T.S.D.
IF SLAVERY WAS A CHOICE, WHAT WAS THE
OTHER OPTIONS TO BE?

FIRST THEY DIDN'T WANT US TO VOTE, THEN
WE WERE COERCED TO BE DEMOCRATS.
THE ONLY THING DEMOCRATS EVER DID FOR
US, WAS GIVE US WELFARE AND CHEESE, AND
TREAT US LIKE RATS.
THEY SENT US OFF TO WAR, TO COME BACK TO
AMERICA, TO BE TREATED LIKE AND CALLED
NIGGER.
WE CONSTANTLY GOT TO TURN THE OTHER
CHEEK, AND BE THE PERSON THAT'S BIGGER.
THEY TREATED US LIKE ANIMALS, SAID WE
WERE ¾ OF HUMAN BEINGS.
BUT THEY KNOW WE ARE GOD'S, QUEENS, AND
KINGS, PRE DATING THE INDO EUROPEANS.

INTROVERTED

 BORN ALONE, DIE ALONE.
STAND FOR SOMETHING, EVEN IF YOU HAVE
TO STAND ALONE.
FOLLOWING THE EASY ROAD, MIGHT NOT BE
MEANT FOR YOU.
TO YOURSELF, YOU MUST ALWAYS REMAIN
TRUE.
QUIETEST PEOPLE HAVE THE LOUDEST MINDS.
WITH A LOT OF PEOPLE, GOOD TIMES WE TRY
TO FIND.
I'M NEVER BORED BY MYSELF.
9 TIMES OUT IF 10, I'D CHOOSE TO BE BY
MYSELF.
I'VE LIVE TO LEARN, YOU HAVE LESS PROBLEMS
WITH LESS PEOPLE.

THE MANIPULATING, OPPRESSING, AND
CONNING PEOPLE DO, TO GET TO THE TOP
LIKE A STEEPLE.
THERE'S NOTHING LIKE PEACE AND
HAPPINESS, I MOSTLY FIND THEM WHEN I'M
ALONE.
MOST PEOPLE WANT TO BE FAMOUS, I'D
RATHER BE UNKNOWN.
FAR AWAY FROM THE NEGATIVE ENERGY AND
VIBES.
BEING AT PEACE WITH MYSELF, IS A FEELING I
CAN'T DESCRIBE.
BEING IN A CROWD, YOU CAN EASILY BE
DIVERTED.
I BE IN MY OWN WORLD, I'M TRULY
INTROVERTED.

IF YOU BELIEVE IN YOURSELF, YOU CAN DO
ANYTHING

IF YOU BELIEVE IN YOURSELF, YOU CAN DO
ANYTHING NO MATTER WHAT ANYONE TELLS
YOU.
EVERYONE HAS DREAMS, SO IT REALLY
BOTHERS ME WHEN SOMEONE DOWN OR
DISCOURAGE SOMEONE FROM
ACHIEVING THEIR PERSONAL DREAMS OR
GOALS.
IF YOU ARE A WEAK MINDED PERSON OR A
FOLLOWER, THE NEGATIVE ENERGY WILL
DETOUR YOU FROM REACHING YOUR GOAL.

TO PREVENT YOURSELF FROM NOT FAILING,
ONLY SURROUND YOURSELF WITH POSITIVE
SUPPORTING FRIENDS AND FAMILY.
SET SHORT TERM GOALS TOWARDS YOUR
MAJOR GOAL.
AN EXAMPLE TO THAT IS IF YOU WANT TO BE
MILLIONAIRE, YOUR NOT GOING TO BECOME
ONE OVERNIGHT.
SET A SHORT TERM GOALS TOWARD YOUR
FIRST 1,000, 10,000, 100,000, AND SO ON UNTIL
YOU REACH YOUR MAJOR GOAL.

AFTER LIFE

AFTER MY SPIRIT TRANSCEND, PLANT MY
REMAINS TO BECOME A TREE OF LIFE.
SO MY BODY AND MOTHER NATURE BECOME
CONNECTED, LIKE HUSBAND AND WIFE.
CREATING SHELTER AND NUTRIENTS FOR THE
WILD LIFE IN NATURE.
FOR ANY LIFE ILLS, I HELP TOO PRODUCE THE
CURE.
POSITIVE VIBRATIONS IN THE ATMOSPHERE, SO
MY SPIRIT WILL FOREVER BE FELT.
HIGHLY ENERGETIC SURROUNDINGS ARE
AROUND ME LIKE A BELT.
FROM THE SUNSHINE TO THE MOONLIGHT, I'LL
FOREVER BE A DELIGHT.
I THRIVE TO INSPIRE, I THRIVE TO ENLIGHT.
MY SOUL WILL TRANSCEND TO THE 5TH
DIMENSION.
ENERGY NEVER DIES, I PRAY I COMPLETE MY
MISSION.

OUT OF THIS GALAXY, TO BE ALIGNED WITH
OTHER STARS.
IT SEEMS LIKE FOREVER AND A DAY, BUT THE
TIME ISN'T THAT FAR.
FANTASIES BECOME REALITY WITH GENUINE
FAITH.
I'LL BE ETERNAL, RETURNING AS A WRAITH.
BEING OF THIS WORLD, PEOPLE BECOME SO
STRIFE.
THESE ARE THINGS I PRAY TO ACQUIRE IN MY
AFTERLIFE.

MANIFEST DESTINY

AS YOU THINK, SO SHALL YOU BECOME.
WHAT'S MEANT TO BE, WILL ALWAYS BE THE
OUTCOME.
IT MIGHT NOT COME AS YOU PLANNED, BUT IT
SURELY WILL BE.
YOU HAVE TO HAVE THE KNOWLEDGE TO
KNOW, SOME ARE TO BLINDED TO SEE.
DON'T BECOME OF THE WORLD, MANIFEST
YOUR OWN DESTINY.
DON'T LET THE NEGATIVE ENERGY DETOUR
YOUR LEGACY.
AS YOU THINK YOU VIBRATE. AS YOU VIBRATE
YOU ATTRACT.
ALWAYS PLAN, PLOT, AND STRATEGIZE,
BEFORE YOU REACT.
THE ALL IS A FREQUENCY, SO STAY IN TUNE.
THE END SEEM SO FAR AWAY, BUT WHEN IT
ARRIVES IT'S SUDDENLY SOON.

A PERSON IS ONLY LIMITED BY THE THOUGHTS
THEY CHOOSE.
IT'S NOT ALL BAD, THERE'S LESSONS TO BE
LEARNED WHEN WE LOSE.
IT YOU CAN THINK IT, YOU CAN BE IT, CLAIM IT
AND IT SHALL BE.
KEEP YOUR THIRD EYE OPEN, SO YOU CAN
CLEARLY SEE.
BEING POSITIVE, BRINGS OUT THE BEST IN ME.
IT ALL STARTS WITH A THOUGHT, THEN
MANIFEST INTO DESTINY.

ABSTRACT

I'M JUST LIVING AND LOVING LIFE.
AVOIDING WORLDLY WAYS, SO I WANT END UP
STRIFE.
KEEPING MY SOUL PROTECTED, FROM THESE
EVIL SPIRITS.
I'M INTROVERTED, SO I JUST PUT MY THOUGHTS
IN LYRICS.
I'M NOT GOING TO LET YOUR LOW
VIBRATIONS, KILL MY VIBE.
TAKE HEED TO THE WORDS THAT I SCRIBE.
WHEN YOU GIVE UP, YOU LOSE.
WE ALL CAN LEARN SOMETHING, GETTING A
PERSPECTIVE FROM A DIFFERENT VIEW.
YOU CEASE TO THINK, WHEN YOU THINK YOU
KNOW IT ALL.
IT'S BEYOND THEIR COMPREHENSION, THAT'S
WHY THEY THINK SO SMALL.

A GENIUS IS ALWAYS BRANDED CRAZY.
OPEN YOUR EYES AND MAY SEE.
LIFE IS AN ART, I'M TRYING TO LIVE A
ENLIGHTEN AND INSPIRATIONAL PICTURE.
AND BE SOMETHING YOU HAVE TO RESORT
BACK TO LIKE A SCRIPTURE.
I'M A MELANATED BEING, TURNING SUNLIGHT
TO ENERGY.
BEFORE I TRANSCEND BACK TO THE 5TH
DIMENSION AND BE A MEMORY.

CONVERSATIONS WITH MY OFFSPRING

IT'S NOTHING MORE JOYFUL THAN HEARING
MY OFFSPRING VOICE.
FOR THE BEST FOR THEM, I ALWAYS HAVE TO
MAKE THE RIGHT CHOICE.
YOU CAN'T TURN BACK THE HANDS OF TIME,
BUT YOU CAN PLAN FOR THE FUTURE.
IT'S ALWAYS ROOM OR IMPROVEMENT, BECOME
BETTER THAN YOU WERE.
I SHARE MY KNOWLEDGE AND EXPERIENCE
FROM MY TIME'S IN MY LIFE.
NOBODY'S PERFECT, TOWARDS FAMILY DON'T
REMAIN STRIFE.
THE FEELING OF YOU KNOWING THEY ARE
HAPPY AND DOING GOOD.
HAVING HEART TO HEART CONVERSATIONS,
BEING UNDERSTOOD.
GIVING THEM ADVICE, HAVING FAITH THEY
MAKE THE RIGHT DECISION.

IT'S ALWAYS FAMILY OVER EVERYTHING, I'M
TRULY BIG ON.
WITNESSING SO THEY CAN DEFEAT ALL THEIR
TRIALS, AND HAVE NO TRIBULATIONS.
I'M LIVING FOR THE LOVE I RECEIVE FROM MY
OFFSPRING CONVERSATIONS.
IT'S A TWO WAY STREET THEY ENLIGHTEN AND
INSPIRE ME TOO.
THE ALL MOST HIGH GREATEST GIFT TO ME IS
MY 3 + 2.
THREE GODDESSES AND TWO SUNS, MAKE MY
LIFE COMPLETE.
EVERY ENTIRE CONVERSATION WE HAVE, I
WISH I COULD TWEET.

IRRITATED DEMONS

YOU NEVER HAVE NOTHING TO SAY, WHEN IT
COME TO MAKING THINGS BETTER.
BUT HAVE SO MUCH TO SAY, WHEN I
SUPPOSEDLY UPSET HER.
YOU TELL LIES SO MUCH, THAT YOU START TO
BELIEVE IN THEM.
THROUGHOUT ALL THE GOOD THAT HAS AND
BEING DONE, YOU TRY TO CONDEMN.
THIS IS SO PETTY AND IGNORANT, THAT I
SHOULDN'T BE ADDRESSING.
I SHOULD BE SOMEWHERE CELEBRATING LIFE,
COUNTING MY BLESSINGS.
BUT I'M VENTING TO THE WORLD, TOO
PREVENT FROM STRESSING.

LIFE IS TOO SHORT, TOO LIVE IT DEPRESSING.
WHEN YOU ARE THE ONE DOING WRONG, IT'S
ALL GOOD.
BUT WHEN THE TABLES TURN, YOU ACT AS IF
YOU NEVER UNDERSTOOD.
KNOWING YOU ARE DEAD WRONG, NOW YOU
WANT TO ACT AS THE VICTIM.
PRAY TO THE MOST HIGH, GET THAT DEVIL
OUT YOUR SYSTEM.
I GOT TO START SPENDING MORE TIME IN THE
SUN.
BECAUSE DEALING WITH THESE
DEGENERATES, GOT ME FEELING BUM.
MY HIGH POSITIVE SPIRIT, SEEMS TO IRRITATE
THEY DEMONS.
IF I CONTINUE TO GIVE THEM MY TIME AND
MY ENERGY, IT WILL GO ON FOR EONS

THIS IS THE THANKS I GET

NO MATTER RIGHT OR WRONG, I ALWAYS
SPOKE HIGHLY IN YOUR FAVOR.
IF IT MEANT SACRIFICE MY LIFE, THAT'S WHAT
I'D DO TO SAVE HER.
WHAT AM I TO EXPECT, IF PEOPLE CAN'T BE
LOYAL TO THEIR SAVIOR.
IT MUST BE SOMETHING IN THE FOOD, THAT'S
CAUSING THE INAPPROPRIATE BEHAVIOR.
UNGRATEFUL, BECAUSE THAT'S ALL IN LIFE
YOU WERE TAUGHT TO BE.
NEVER LEARN ON HOW TO AGREE TO
DISAGREE.

I'M TRYING TO HOLD ON TO YOU, BUT IT'S BEST
TO BECOME AN AMPUTEE.
WE'LL NEVER HAVE NOTHING, IF WE CAN'T
HAVE TRUST AND LOYALTY.
I GAVE YOU MY ALL AND THIS IS THE THANKS
THAT I GET.
I DID IT FROM MY HEART, YOU ARE NOT IN MY
DEBT.
I'M EMBEDDED IN YOUR MIND, ME, YOU'LL
NEVER FORGET.
AND I GUARANTEE, I DON'T PLACE NO BETS.
IT'S SAID THAT, "WHAT DOESN'T KILL YOU,
ONLY MAKE YOU STRONG."
IT SEEMS LIKE, I'M A MAGNET TO THE
HEADSTRONG.
IS THERE A SUCH THING AS PERFECT, IF NOT,
HOW COULD IT BE WRONG?
PROBLEMS IN OUR LIFE, SEEMS TO BE
LIFELONG.

DIE 4 U

THEN; I WAS LIVING FOR THE LOVE OF YOU,
NOW; I WOULD DIE 4 U.
IF YOU SOLELY PAY ATTENTION, I'M GIVING
YOU CUE.
I'M WAY OUT OF SYNC, BECAUSE I REMAIN TOO
STAY TRUE.
IF IT ISN'T GOOD FOR MY SOUL, I DON'T NEED
NOTHING NEW.

REQUIRED POSITIVE ENERGY AND
VIBRATIONS, LIFE'S TOO SHORT TO ALWAYS
REMAIN BLUE.
LESS PEOPLE LESS PROBLEMS, I NEVER RAN
WITH A CREW.
IT'S EMBEDDED IN MY ROOTS, NEVER DO WHAT
THEY DO.
I'M JUST LIVING MY LIFE, THE NEXT MAN I'M
NOT TRYING TO OUTDO.
WHAT'S GOOD FOR ME, MAY NOT BE GOOD FOR
YOU.
IS YOUR LEGACY GOING TO BE HAVING
MATERIALISTIC ITEMS WITH NO MONETARY
VALUE.
OR IS YOUR LEGACY GOING TO BE FROM THE
THINGS THAT YOU DO.
YOU GOT TO LIVE WITH THE DECISIONS YOU
MAKE, LIFE YOU CAN'T UNDO.
DON'T FOREVER REMAIN THE STUDENT,
THRIVE TO BE THE GURU.
I SAY SO MUCH, WITH SAYING SO LITTLE LIKE A
HAIKU.
ASK IF YOU DON'T UNDERSTAND, WORDS
COULD BE EASILY MISCONSTRUE.

THOUGHTS OF THE DAY

AS LONG YOU AS YOUR ALIVE TOO SEE
ANOTHER DAY, YOU HAVE ANOTHER CHANCE.
STOP LIVING RETRO, AND START LIVING IN
ADVANCE.

I'M TOO BUSY RIGHT NOW, SO I TOLD HER SAVE
THE LAST DANCE.
THE D THAT GOES IN THE BANK, IS THE ONLY
ONE I'M TRYING TO ENHANCE.
TIME IS PRICELESS, THAN IT'S FOLLOWED BY
FINANCE.
WHATEVER YOU BELIEVE IN, NEVER FOLD
ALWAYS KEEP YOUR STANCE.
GET A GOOD LOOK, YOU'D MISS OUT IF YOU
GLANCE.
WHEN THEY FINALLY COMPREHEND, I'LL HAVE
THEM IN A TRANCE.
I THRIVE TO NOT MAKE MY LIFE AN
UNFORTUNATE CIRCUMSTANCE.
YOUR VISION IS TOO NARROW, YOUR MIND
YOU NEED TOO EXPANSE.
I'M A BIG STEPPER, ALL YOU DO IS PRANCE.
IT WAS BOUND TO HAPPEN IT WASN'T BY
PERCHANCE.
I HAVE TO BE DESTINED, MY BIRTH WAS
HAPPENSTANCE.
WE ARE STILL MODERN DAY SLAVES, DECEIVED
THINKING WE FREELANCE.
SPREADING POSITIVE VIBES, MAKE THESE
DEMONS LOOK ASKANCE.
I'M SO NICE, YOU'D THINK I'M IN THE SOUTH
OF FRANCE.

CUE INTELLIGENCE

EVERYTHING I'VE WRITTEN IS THE MOST HIGH
GIVEN, NOT ARTIFICIAL INTELLIGENCE.
TRUE ARTIST AREN'T TRULY EMBRACE UNTIL
THEY'RE DEAD, SO I EXPECT THE NEGLIGENCE.
OUT OF SITE, OUT OF MIND, SO I PRACTICE
ABSTINENCE.
YOU LIVED YOUR WHOLE LIFE COMPLIANT,
WITH NO SUBSTANCE.
CRITICAL THINKING IS A RARE TRAIT.
LOVE ISN'T REAL, THE MOTIVATION IS HATE.
IT'S BEYOND MY CONTROL, SOME SAY IT'S FATE.
DEATH IS APART OF LIVING, WE ALL MUST
AWAIT.
THEY SAY IT'S NEVER TO LATE, THAT'S TRULY A
LIE.
IT TAKES TWO, BUT ONLY ONE OF US APPLY.
IT'S IN THE MOST HIGH HANDS, I DON'T HAVE
TO WISH THAT YOU DIE.
I'M SURE YOU WILL RETURN, I'M NOT SURE I'LL
STANDBY.
WE SURELY WOULD OF ACCOMPLISHED, IF
THAT WAS THE INTENTION.
THROUGHOUT ALL THE DRAMA IN MY LIFE, I
STILL FIND CIRCUMVENTION.
I'LL ALWAYS THINK BEFORE I ACT, LIFE'S CHESS
NOT CHECKERS.
IT'S KNOWN TO BUST PIPES, BUT DIAMONDS
ARE ALSO FORMED UNDER PRESSURE.

ACTIONS

EVERY ACTION DOESN'T DESERVE A
REACTION.
STAY FOCUS, DON'T GET DETOURED BY THE
DISTRACTION.
IT'S RARELY WORTHY OF TIME, IF IT DOESN'T
CALL FOR A CURRENCY TRANSACTION.
WORDS CAN BE LOUD BUT NOT CLEAR, IF THEY
AREN'T MATCHING YOUR ACTIONS.
SAYING NOTHING, IS MOSTLY ALWAYS SAYING
SOMETHING.
IT COULD HAVE BEEN GOING ON FOREVER,
BUT SOMETIMES IT COULD BE THAT ONE
THING.
THEY MAKE IT LOOK SO GOOD AND REAL, LIKE
SOME BIGEN.
THE TRUTH ALWAYS COMES OUT, WHEN THEY
START RAGING.
THINGS COULD BE ALL SO SIMPLE, BUT THEY
RATHER MAKE IT HARD.
NOWADAYS YOUR LOOKED AT AS ODD, IF YOU
ARE NOT A RETARD.
IMAGINE THE TROUBLE YOU'D BE IN, IF YOU
DIDN'T KNOW HOW TO DISREGARD.
SOMETHINGS YOU GO THROUGH IN LIFE,
LEAVE YOU FOREVER SCARRED.
FOR EVERY ACTION, THERE'S AN EQUAL OR
OPPOSITE REACTION.
LIFE WILL STILL BE GREAT, IF WE NEVER HAVE
ANOTHER INTERACTION.
I DEAL IN WHOLE, I'M NOT GOOD WITH
FRACTIONS.

YOU ARE JUST NOW REALIZING, BUT IT BEEN
INACTION

IT TAKES A VILLAGE

I WANT TO THANK THE VILLAGE THAT HELP
RAISED MY CHILDREN.
THANKS FOR GUIDING THEM RIGHT, IN THIS
WORLD FULL OF SIN.
FROM THE GRANDPARENTS TO THE AUNT,
UNCLES, COUSIN, AND FRIENDS OF FAMILY.
YOUR CONTRIBUTIONS ARE PRICELESS, THERE
NOTHING I CAN PAY YOU BACK AS
BENEFICIALLY.
THERE'S NO WORDS FOR DESCRIBING THE
FEELINGS I HAVE FOR YOU ALL.
I'D SACRIFICE MY LIFE IF NEEDED, IF I EVER
GOT THAT CALL.
KNOWING MY CHILDREN ARE GOOD, I CAN
TRANSCEND PEACEFULLY.
EVEN THOUGH I'M TRYING TO LIVE AND BE
THERE FOR ETERNITY.
THANKS FOR THE LOVE, TIME,
ENLIGHTENMENT, AND INSPIRATION.
IT WANT BE IN VAIN, ONCE THEY REACH THEIR
DESTINATION.
I'M SURE THEY WOULD CARRY ON ALL OF OUR
LEGACIES.
IT WAS BOUND TO BE, IT WAS WRITTEN BY THE
PROPHECIES.
EVEN WITH THE VILLAGE BEING SEGREGATED,
THE MOST HIGH STILL MADE A WAY.

NO WEAPON FORMED PROSPERED, EVEN WHEN
SATAN TRY TO DISARRAY.
I LOVE YOU ALL FROM THE BOTTOM OF MY
HEART.
YOUR ACTIONS ARE PRICELESS, FOR DOING
MORE THAN YOUR PART.

BETRAYAL

BETRAYED BY THOSE I LOVE MOST,
UNLOYAL DEEDS THAT HURT AND BOAST.
BUT I WON'T LET THEIR ACTIONS WIN,
MY STRENGTH WILL RISE, I'M MADE OF THICK
SKIN.
LOVE CANNOT LIVE WHERE THERE IS NO
TRUST,
WITH TIME COME CHANGE, I ADAPT, I ADJUST.
UNKNOWN BETRAYAL CAN'T HOLD ME DOWN,
I'LL SOAR ABOVE WITH A VICTOR'S CROWN.
LESSONS IN LIFE CAN BE HARD,
BUT THEY MAKE US WHO WE ARE.
TRIALS AND TESTS ARE PART OF THE PLAN,
FOR GROWTH AND WISDOM TO BE GAINED.
CHERISH THE MOMENTS, TREASURE THE
MEMORIES,
OR IT'S JUST TIME SPENT IN VAIN, FORGOTTEN
ANNIVERSARIES .
FOR TIME IS FLEETING, AND LIFE IS BUT A
DANCE.
NOBODY'S PERFECT, EVERYONE DESERVES A
CHANCE.

EMBRACE THE JOURNEY, LEARN FROM THE
PAST,
AND LET YOUR HEART GUIDE YOU TO YOUR
FUTURE AT LAST.

LIFE LESSON

DISCOVERING TRUTH BEYOND THE VEIL,
TRYING TO STAY RIGHTEOUS, TO AVOID HELL.
UNTANGLING THOUGHTS THAT MAKE ONE
FRAIL,
STAYING PRAYED UP, SO I CAN PREVAIL.
ILLUMINATED BY THE LIGHT WITHIN,
TRYING TO BALANCE THE YANG AND THE YIN.
EMBRACING PEACE AND SHEDDING SIN.
TRYING TO MAKE THE BEST DECISION, SO I
WANT HAVE TO REPEAT AGAIN.
THE JOURNEY TOWARDS ENLIGHTENMENT,
AVOIDING BECOMING A PRODUCT OF THE
ENVIRONMENT.
A QUEST THAT FREES THE MIND'S
CONFINEMENT,
LIFE IS A TEST, I'M TRYING TO PASS ALL
ASSIGNMENTS.
LIFE'S MYSTERIES, NO LONGER A PLIGHT,
I'LL NEVER GIVE UP, OR GO OUT WITHOUT A
FIGHT.
BEING ILLUMINATED, I SHINE LIKE THE LIGHT.
THIRD EYE ACTIVE, BRIGHTENED BY
NEWFOUND INSIGHT.

THIRD EYE OPEN

THE THIRD EYE AWAKENS
KNOWING THE TRUTH FROM ACCUSATIONS
A VISION WAY BEYOND THE SEEN
SOMETHINGS CAN'T BE TAUGHT, ITS ALL IN
THE GENES
THE TRUTH ALWAYS LIES WITHIN
WHILE YOU ARE TRYING TO FIGURE IT OUT,
YOU GOT TO BEGIN
FROM REALITY, PERCEIVING A DIFFERENT
DREAM.
REJECT WORLDLY WAYS, LIVE TO REDEEM.
AWARENESS WE MUST AMPLIFYING.
RISE AGAIN, AFTER THEY CRUCIFY.
A NEW BEGINNING, WHEN A NEW PERSPECTIVE
STARTS .
YOU GOT TO HAVE A VISION, LIFE IS AN ART.
LIVE TO BE AN ASSET, AVOID LIABILITIES .
OPEN YOUR MIND, TO THE INFINITE
POSSIBILITIES.
KEEP YOUR THOUGHTS BEYOND AND AFAR .
WHEN CHAKRAS ARE ALIGNED, & THE THIRD
EYE IS AJAR.

FLOWER OF LIFE

PETALS SPREADING IN EVERY DIRECTION,
THROUGH THE PATTERN OF LIFE, WE HAVE A
CONNECTION.
A PERFECT HARMONY, NO IMPERFECTION.

WHEN WE TRANSCEND, WILL WE HAVE A
RESURRECTION.
ALL LIFE IS CONNECTED, BOUND BY ITS FORM,
MOST PEOPLE ARE LOST BY BEING MISINFORM.
MAKING LIFE'S NATURAL PATTERN TO BE
DEFORM.
THE SACRED SYMBOL, A FLOWER OF LIFE IS
BORN.
ETERNAL AND INFINITE, A CONSTANT
RENEWAL,
REMAIN POSITIVE IN THIS WORLD THAT'S
CRUEL.
WHEN YOUR ENERGY GET LOW, FIND AWAY TO
REFUEL.
A NEVER-ENDING CYCLE, A UNIVERSAL JEWEL.

HAPPY FATHER'S DAY

ON THIS DAY OF MY REIGN,
IT'S ALL JOY, I'M BLOCKING OUT THE PAIN.
NO MATTER WHAT, MY LOVE WILL ALWAYS
SUSTAIN,
GUIDED BY MY HEART, FOLLOWED BY MY
BRAIN.
A PILLAR OF SUPPORT THAT WILL NEVER WANE,
I'M DESTINE TO BE ABLE, BUT SOME DAYS I
FEEL LIKE I'M CAIN.
PREFORMING MY DUTIES, I'M NOT A HERO
WITH UTMOST ACCLAIM,
MY LOVE IS CONSTANT AND NEVER IN VAIN,

SACRIFICE MY LIFE AND REFUSE TO COMPLAIN
MY GUIDANCE AND WISDOM WE'LL ALWAYS
RETAIN,
SEEING MY KIDS BE HAPPY, IS ALL I'M TRYING
TO OBTAIN.
LIFE'S IN NEED OF SUN, AS MUCH AS RAIN
LOVE, PEACE, AND HAPPINESS, WE THRIVE TO
ATTAIN.
CONNECTED THROUGH THE ALL MOST HIGH,
SO WE'LL ALWAYS REMAIN.
WHEN I TRANSCEND, THEY'LL CARRY ON THE
REIGN.
HAPPY FATHER'S DAY, FOREVERMORE AGAIN.

JUNETEENTH

JUNETEENTH, A DAY TO CELEBRATE.
FROM ACTIONS OF HUMANS THAT'S
INVERTEBRATES.
EMANCIPATION, FREEDOM FOR THE
ENSLAVED.
NO REPARATIONS FOR THE INVOLUNTARY
RIGHTS THAT'S BEEN WAIVED.
RED, WHITE, BLUE—THE COLORS WE ARE
FORCED TO FLY.
STANDING FOR RED, BLACK, AND GREEN ARE
THE REASON WE DIE
CHAINS BROKEN, HOPE CAN NOW REVIVE.
THEY NEVER ADDRESS WHERE THE PROBLEMS
DERIVE.

A NATION'S PROMISE, LONG OVERDUE.
BECAUSE OF THE MISTREATMENT FOR YOUR
SKIN HUE.
HONORING ANCESTORS, THEIR STRUGGLES
TRUE.
KNOWING BETTER, BETTER WE WOULD DO.
"NOBODY'S FREE UNTIL EVERYBODY'S FREE."
THEY SEE US ALL THE SAME, POOR, RICH, OR
BOURGEOISIE.
HISTORY BRIEFLY TOLD TO BE MISCONSTRUED.
MEMORIES OF RESILIENCE, FOREVER IMBUED.

AT PEACE

ACCEPTANCE BRINGS SERENITY,
CHAKRAS ALIGNED THE RESULTS AMENITY.
MIND AND SOUL IN HARMONY,
THIRD EYE OPEN, IT'S THE GOD IN ME.
NO MORE STRUGGLES TO BE FREE,
IF I TRANSCEND TODAY, LIVES ON MY ENERGY.
CONTENT WITH WHO I AM TO BE.
TRIALS AND TRIBULATIONS OPEN MY EYES TO
SEE.
TRANQUILITY FLOWS LIKE A STREAM,
THE DECEPTION OF PERCEPTION,
EVERYTHING ISN'T WHAT IT SEEM.
AN INNER CALM, A PEACEFUL DREAM,
KNOWING THYSELF I'M FULL OF SELF ESTEEM.
GRATEFUL FOR THIS BLESSED THEME,
THE MOST HIGH DON'T MAKE MISTAKES, I
WOULDN'T TRADE AANYTHING.
I'M LIVING LIFE TO THE EXTREME.
I'M AT PEACE WITH MYSELF, IT IS WHAT IT
SEEMS.

BROADEN YOUR HORIZONS

YOU DWELL IN SHALLOW THOUGHTS EACH
DAY,
COMPLAINING ABOUT A PROBLEM, INSTEAD OF
FINDING A WAY.
EXPAND YOUR MIND, AND DON'T DELAY.
ALWAYS REMAIN FOCUS, DON'T LET DRAMA
STEER YOU ASTRAY.
THERE'S MUCH TO LEARN BEYOND YOUR
SCOPE,
DON'T BECOME STAGNATE, LIKE YOU STUCK
ON DOPE.
SO TAKE THE LEAP, AND DON'T LOSE HOPE.
PURSUE TO OVER ACHIEVE, DON'T JUST COPE.
BROADEN YOUR HORIZONS THE MORE YOU
SEE.
ANYTHING YOU PUT YOUR MIND TOO, YOU
CAN BE.
THE WORLD IS VAST; IT'S YOUR DECREE.
NEVER DELAY, GET IT DONE A.S.A.P.
DON'T THINK TOO SHALLOW; ALWAYS
ELEVATE.
START TO WORRY, WHEN THEY DON'T HATE.
CREATE YOUR OWN AGENDA, CONTROL YOUR
OWN FATE.
ALWAYS THINK DEEP, AND SUCCESS WILL
AWAIT.

PHASE IX

LIFE

UNGRATEFUL

UNGRATEFUL HEARTS, THAT'S COLD AS ICE,
THEIR ATTITUDE, DISREGARD ALL THE TIMES
YOU WAS NICE.
NEVER SEEING OR KNOWING THE SACRIFICE,
ENVIOUS PERSON DISCOMBOBULATING THEM
WITH BAD ADVICE.
BLINDED BY THEIR OWN DESIRE,
NEVER PUTTING THEIR FEET IN YOUR SHOES
TO ACQUIRE.
IGNORING THOSE WHO NEVER TIRE.
KNOWING THE TRUTH, STILL SIDING WITH A
LIAR.
TURNING AWAY FROM LOVE AND CARE,
FROM THEIR PAST ACTIONS, YOU WERE ALWAYS
AWARE.
THROUGH EXPERIENCES, WE REALIZE LIFE
ISN'T FAIR.
LOVE SUSTAIN YOUR FAITH, EVEN AFTER YOU
SWEAR.
THE PURSUIT OF HAPPINESS AND PEACE.
THEY ONLY KNOW HOW TO SHOW LOVE, WHEN
YOU DECEASE.
BUT WHEN YOUR BLESSINGS SEEM TO COME TO
A CEASE,
THEY FINALLY REALIZE WHAT THEY
RELEASED.

WHITE PRIVILEGE

WHITE PRIVILEGE, BORN IN SKIN,
NO MATTER HOW WRONG I AM, I'M STILL
GOING TO WIN.
A VEIL OF COMFORT, WRAPPED WITHIN,
IT'S A WHITE MAN WORLD, NOTHING WE DO IS
A SIN.
A LIFE OF EASE, OFTEN UNSEEN,
TO LET IT BE KNOWN, I TATTOO THE 13.
SYSTEMIC ADVANTAGE, A CONSTANT THEME.
YOU KNOW ABOUT IT, AND STILL CAN'T DO A
THING.
BLIND TO STRUGGLE, DEAF TO STRIFE,
NON WHITE, YOUR HEAVEN IS IN THE
AFTERLIFE.
ENTRENCHED ADVANTAGES, RIFE WITH LIFE,
MELANATED PEOPLE GET LOOKED UPON LIKE
WILDLIFE.
INHERENT BIASES, FOSTERED BY LIGHT,
WE'LL TELL A WHITE LIE, TO MAKE OUR
WRONG RIGHT.
ACTIONS WE ARE HONORED FOR, MIGHT GET
YOU INDICT.
A PRIVILEGE HELD, IN PLAIN SIGHT.

DEAD TO ME

YOU'RE NOTHING BUT A MEMORY,
THE LOVE WILL NEVER REKINDLE, YOUR DEAD
TO ME.
IT IS WHAT IT IS, NO COGNITION, TO WHAT IT
COULD BE.
YOUR TO BROKEN TO PAY ATTENTION, I'LL
LOWER THE FEE.
TO HATE ME, YOU GOT TO HATE YOURSELF.
PAY ME BACK FOR MY SUPPORT AND GET OFF
MY SELF.
YOU'RE DEAD TO ME, A DISTANT PAST.
YOU HAVE A DULL FUTURE, I PRAY YOU LAST.
I'VE MOVED ON FROM YOUR MISERY,
YOU ARE A LOST CHILD, I PRAY FOR YOUR
RECOVERY.
MY HEART'S NO LONGER IN YOUR GRASP.
BEING LOST AND CONFUSED, YOU SOUND SO
RASP.
ALL THE FAIL ATTEMPTS, YOU TRIED TO BRING
ME DOWN,
MY HEAD IS STILL UP, INTACT WITH A CROWN.
AS YOU SEE, I ROSE ABOVE IT ALL.
TEN TOES DOWN, I REMAIN TO STAND TALL.
NOW I WEAR MY VICTORY CROWN,
ENTERTAIN BY YOUR FOOLISHNESS, YOU'RE A
TRUE CLOWN.
I REMAIN ABOVE LIKE THE MOST HIGH OF ALL.
AS YOU REMAIN AN ABOMINATION, THINKING
FOREVER SMALL.

CUE INTUITION BEFORE LEAVING EARTH

CUE INTUITION BEFORE LEAVING EARTH.
POURING OUT MY SOUL, FROM THE TIME OF MY
BIRTH.
DIVINE WHISPERS GUIDE MY WORTH.
WHEN MY THIRD OPENED WAS MY REBIRTH.
SUBLIME ENERGY IGNITES THE FLAME.
GRADE A CUE, MY NAME IS MY NAME.
TRUST THE UNIVERSE, IT'S NOT A GAME.
I'M TRYING TO LEAVE A LEGACY FOR MY KIDS
TO PROCLAIM.
LET FAITH BE YOUR COMPASS, NOT FEAR.
I'M NOT TRYING TO BE A PRODUCT OF
SOCIETY, DOING THE SAME THING EVERY
YEAR.
OUR JOURNEY ENDS BUT WE PERSEVERE.
POSITIVE ENERGY AND VIBRATIONS PRESENT
WHEN I APPEAR.
EMBRACE THE UNKNOWN, WITH OPEN HEARTS.
BETTERING YOURSELF IS WHERE IT ALL STARTS.
PURSUING TO MAKE IT SWEET, WHEN LIFE GET
TART.
CUE INTUITION AND LIFE IMPARTS.

TRYING TO SURVIVE, WE FORGET WHAT WE
ARE LIVING FOR.

FIGHTING TO STAY ALIVE EACH DAY,
LIVING FOR THE BILLS THAT WE PAY.
SUCCUMBING TO THE PRESSURES OF FRAY.
CONTINUOUSLY WISHING FOR A GET AWAY.
FORGETTING OUR PURPOSE, OUR REASON,
NEW TRIALS AND TRIBULATIONS EACH SEASON.
IN THIS CONSTANT BATTLE, IT'S TREASON.
MAKING OTHERS HAPPY, BUT MYSELF I'M NOT
PLEASING.
WE MUST REMEMBER WHAT WE'RE STRIVING
TOWARD,
WHILE KEEPING OUR MIND AND BODY ON ONE
ACCORD.
LEST WE LOSE SIGHT AND BECOME BORED.
IT'S SAD AFTER WE DIE, WE GET THE REWARD.
ENLIGHTEN TO SURVIVE FOR SOMETHING
BIGGER,
REMAINING AN OUTCAST, I DON'T WANT TO BE
JUST ANOTHER N!66@.
I'M AT BAT, LIFE'S THE PITCHER.
BEING HEALTHY AND ALIVE, THAT WHAT
MAKES LIFE RICHER.

DISCOMBOBULATED

A WANDERING SOUL IN SEARCH OF YOURSELF,
PRAYING ONE DAY YOUR ENLIGHTEN TO
KNOW THYSELF.
AMIDST THE CHAOS, YOUR ALL ALONE,
SOME THINGS ARE BEYOND YOUR

UNDERSTANDING, UNTIL YOU GET GROWN.
RECKLESSLY DIRECTIONLESS WITHOUT A CLUE,
CROSS CERTAIN LINES, YOU KNOW WHAT IT
WILL COME TOO.
LOST AND CONFUSED NOT KNOWING WHAT
YOU SHOULD DO?
SOON YOU WILL WAKE UP & HAVE A CLEAR
VIEW.
RIGHT NOW YOUR MIND IS TOO JUMBLED,
THOUGHTS UNCLEAR,
BEST BELIEVE, THINGS AREN'T ALWAYS WHAT
THEY SEEM TO APPEAR.
FEELING LOST, FILLED WITH SO MUCH FEAR,
MY HEART IS SO NUMB, I CAN'T SHED A TEAR.
IN THIS MAZE OF LIFE, YOUR FEELING SO
TRAPPED,
IF YOU NEVER GROW, YOU'D NEVER ADAPT.
YOU NEED TO TAKE SOME TIME, TO THINK
BACK THEN RECAP.
AND REALIZE THE REAL, FROM ALL THAT CAP.

MY HEART SPEAKING

MY LOVE FOR YOU RUNS SO DEEP AND TRUE,
FOLLOWING MY HEART, I TEND TO OVERDO.
MY ENERGY ALWAYS POSITIVE, PLUS MY
VIBRATIONS TOO.
THESE FEELINGS I HAVE I CANNOT ESCHEW.
EVERY MOMENT SPENT WITH YOU IS SO
GRAND,
WITH YOU IN MY PRESENCE LIGHT UP MY
PINEAL GLAND.

YOU ARE A MIRACLE, THIS HAS TO BE THE MOST
HIGH PLAN.
HAVING YOU BY MY SIDE, I PRAY WE NEVER
DISBAND.
I'M TRYING TO FIND THE WORDS, TO BEST
DESCRIBE THESE FEELINGS.
HEAVEN MUST BE LIKE THE TIMES WHEN WE
HAVE DEALINGS.
WHEN WE'RE TOGETHER, OUR LIMITS ARE WAY
BEYOND THE CEILINGS.
OUR CONVERSATIONS ARE COMPATIBLE TO
SEXUAL HEALINGS.
YOU LIGHT UP MY WORLD WITH YOUR GENTLE
SPARK,
WITHOUT YOU IN MY WORLD, IT'S TRULY DARK.
YOU HAVE A BODY OF A GODDESS, PLUS
DIVINELY SMART.
I'M GRATEFUL FOR YOU, MY LOVE, MY HEART.

AFFIRMATIVE ACTION

COLOR BLIND, YET CONSCIOUS OF EACH HUE,
THE MELANATED GET OVER PENALIZED, FOR
THE ACTIONS THEY DO.
THROUGH REALMS OF MERIT, EQUITY'S DEBUT,
MARGINALIZED BY STEREOTYPES THAT AREN'T
TRUE.
SIFT THROUGH THE SEEDS OF OPPORTUNITY,
LOOK AT THIS COUNTRY'S PROGRESS WITH THE
DISUNITY.
DISMANTLING BARRICADES, UNLOCKING
UNITY,

WHEN THE PANDEMIC CAME, WE ALL NEEDED
IMMUNITY.
WIDENING PATHS FOR THE MARGINALIZED
FEW,
THE MELANATED GOT TO WORK 10 TIMES
HARDER THAN THEY DO.
AFFIRMING THE TRUTH, JUSTICE RINGS TRUE,
IN FEAR OF OUR PROGRESS, IF WE WASN'T
SUBDUE.
INCLUSIVE STRIDES GAINED UNDER SHARED
SKIES,
THE BEAUTIFUL WORLD THIS WOULD BE, IF WE
ALL ARISE.
I'LL CONTINUE TO FIGHT FOR AFFIRMATIVE
ACTION UNTIL MY DEMISE.
TOGETHER, EQUALITY'S WINGS SHALL RISE.

INDEPENDENCE DAY

THE SKY BURSTS BRIGHT WHITE, BLUE, AND
RED,
"FREEDOM ISN'T FREE", IS BEST SAID.
BLAZING WITH PATRIOTIC PASSION.
TO THIS DAY, PEOPLE OF AFRICAN DECENT
RECEIVES NO COMPASSION.
FLAGS WAVE AND HEARTS ARE LED.
WE FOUGHT FOR THIS COUNTRY, SO THE
POLICE CAN KILL US DEAD.
TO CELEBRATE OUR NATION'S FASHION.
TO BE GIVING NO RESPECT OR NO
COMPASSION.

FREEDOM RINGS IN EVERY HEAD.
EVERY MOVEMENT WE CREATED WAS
INFILTRATED BY THE FEDS.
WITH A UNITY OF PROGRESSION.
IT'S THE AMERICAN WAY, MELANATED PEOPLE
OPPRESSION.
HAPPY INDEPENDENCE DAY, WE SAID,
OUR ANCESTORS WAS STILL IN THE FIELD,
GETTING HUNG DEAD.
NOT HATED BY ACTIONS, BUT OUR
COMPLEXION.
WITH AN INTENSE FERVOR OF AFFECTION.

NO GOOD DEEDS GOES UNPUNISHED

IN SHADOWS DWELLS A MOURNFUL TRUTH,
IT WILL COME TO THE LIGHT, EVEN IF YOU
AREN'T SLEUTH.
NO GOOD DEED, IT SEEMS, FINDS RESPITE.
YOU SEE WHO THEY TRULY ARE, WHEN THEY
AREN'T DESPERATE.
FOR KINDNESS SOWN, CHAOS TAKES ROOT,
WHEN YOU'RE NO LONGER BENEFICIAL, THEY
GIVE YOU THE BOOT.
LIKE PLAYFUL FIREFLIES IN THE NIGHT.
TO SOME PEOPLE, IT SEEMS LIKE A SIN TO DO
RIGHT.
A GENEROUS HEART, THOUGH PURE AND
BRIGHT,
BUT WITH UNGRATEFUL PEOPLE, YOU ALWAYS
HAVE TO FIGHT.

IS BOUND TO FEEL PAIN, BUT DOES NOT CEASE.
SOME PEOPLE ARE JUST BETTER OFF DECEASE.
YET IN BLESSED ACTS, WE FIND OUR PEACE,
BEING IN TUNED WITH THE MOST HIGH, OUR
BLESSINGS WILL ALWAYS INCREASE.
I CONTINUE TO TAKE IT ALL IN STRIDE.
AND SWALLOW THE BITTER PILL WITH PRIDE.

MAKE AMERICA GREAT AGAIN

MAKE AMERICA GREAT, ONCE UPON A TIME,
A NATION BUILT ON INHUMANE CRIMES.
IMAGINE US BEING TOGETHER SUBLIME.
LIFE WOULD ALWAYS BE IN A PRIME.
UNITE OUR HEARTS, HAND IN HAND,
THINKING THAT DEEP, IS BEYOND MOST TO
UNDERSTAND.
SIDE BY SIDE, WE'LL MAKE OUR STAND.
ALIGNED WITH THE STARS, IN TUNE WITH GOD
PLAN.
WITH HOPE AND STRENGTH, WE'LL REBUILD,
EVERY LEADER OF A CHANGE FOR THE BETTER
MOVEMENT, GET KILLED.
INJUSTICE AND HATRED WE SHALL SHIELD.
IT'S IN THE DNA OF THOSE WHO WERE FORCED
OUT IN THE FIELDS.
A BRIGHTER FUTURE, WE' WILL ATTAIN,
REWARDED FOR MAKING THROUGH THOSE
LIFETIMES, REMAINING SANE.
LOVE, PEACE, AND HAPPINESS, WE WILL
RETAIN.
ONE NATION, ONE LOVE, UNITED, AMERICA
SHALL REGAIN.

SELF DISCIPLINE

INWARD STRENGTH, A GUIDING LIGHT,
MENTALLY PREPARED TO EXPAND MY MIGHT.
CONTROLLED DESIRES, TAKEN FLIGHT,
ONE DAY AT A TIME, NOTHING GREAT
HAPPENS OVERNIGHT.
RESTRAINT ENFOLDS, A STEADY GAZE,
LIVING LIFE CAUGHT UP IN WORLDLY WAYS,
EVERYDAY SPENT TRYING TO ESCAPE THE
MAZE.
PRECIOUS TIME WASTED, GOING THROUGH A
PHASE.
TO BUSY THRIVING TO BE AMAZE.
SOLID STRUCTURE BUILT IN TIMELY WAYS.
AMBITION BURNS, THE FUEL TO STRIVE,
IN GOOD HEALTH, WHAT A TIME TO BE ALIVE.
THROUGH SELF-DISCIPLINE, I WILL CONTINUE
TO THRIVE.
TO LIVE LIFE TO THE FULLEST, AS I SURVIVE.
BALANCE FOUND, IN THIS SACRED TRANCE,
STAYING DISCIPLINE, FOR MENTAL AND
PHYSICAL ADVANCE.
I GIVE MY ALL, EVERY TIME I GET A CHANCE.
CONTROLLED FREEDOM, MY FEARLESS DANCE.

WHITE LIES

HONEST FAÇADES, SHIELDED TRUTHS REMAIN,
WHEN YOU EXPOSE THE TRUTH, THEY MAKE
YOU SEEM INSANE.
GOSSAMER VEILS, DELICATE WHISPERS FEIGN,
THEY FOOL THEMSELVES, THINKING OTHERS
DON'T USE THEIR BRAINS.
WORDS AS SOFT AS SNOW, FREEZING ANSWERS
TAME,
BRAINWASHED AND CONDITIONED TO THINK
THEY ARE THE SMARTEST, BUT THEY'RE
REALLY LAME.
EYES AVERTED, MURKY TRUTHS STAINED,
DEVILS THAT LOSE THEMSELVES, TO HAVE THE
WHOLE WORLD GAINED.
A PALETTE OF DECEIT, SPLATTERED PURE
WHITE,
EVERYTHING WAS DARK BEFORE, "THEN
THERE WAS LIGHT."
FACADES SPUN, ILLUSIONS CAST JUST RIGHT,
ERASED THE TRUE HISTORY, OR EITHER
REWRITE.
A COWARDLY SAVAGE CULTURE, ALL THEY
KNOW IS WAR AND FIGHT.
LOVE TO MAKE OTHERS SUFFER OUT OF SPITE.
KNOWING THEIR GENES ARE RECESSIVE,
CAUSE A BIG FRIGHT.
IN WHITE LIES WE HIDE, TRUTH ENTWINED
TOO TIGHT.

MENTALLY ILL

CHAINS THAT BIND THE MIND'S TERRAIN,
LOOKING FOR DIFFERENT RESULTS, DOING
THE SAME THING OVER AND OVER AGAIN.
DISRUPTING PEACE, CAUSING PAIN,
WILL BLOCK THEIR OWN BLESSINGS, TOO
MAKE SURE YOURS AREN'T OBTAIN.
NO CHOICE BUT TO BEAR THE STRAIN,
THOUGHTS CROSS MY MIND, TO BLOW OUT
YOUR BRAINS.
TRAPPED IN CHAOS AND INSANE.
YOU BETTER OFF WITH A PS5, BECAUSE I'M NOT
THE ONE FOR PLAYING.
WITH HOPE AND HELP, WE CAN REGAIN,
OR I'LL RESPECTFULLY GO LAY DOWN, AFTER
BEING ARRAIGN.
IT'S ALWAYS DRAMA WITH ANYTHING YOU
HAVE TO PERTAIN.
I PROBABLY WANT ENCOUNTER PEACE, UNTIL
YOU ARE SLAIN.
THE LIGHT THAT SHONE, ONCE AGAIN,
IT WILL BE NEXT LIFETIME, FOR OUR
RELATIONSHIP TO BE RETAIN.
THESE PROBABLY WASN'T THE RESULTS, YOU
WERE TRYING TO ATTAIN.
JUST KNOW YOUR MENTAL HEALTH ISSUES IS
NOT IN VAIN.

NOBODY CARES

NOBODY CARES, OR SO IT SEEMS,
NOWADAYS PEOPLE USE A CAPITAL I WHILE
SPELLING TEAM.
IN A WORLD FILLED WITH BROKEN DREAMS.
PEOPLE ARE RARELY STRAIGHT UP, EVERYONE
HAS A SCHEME.
LOST IN A SEA OF APATHY,
FORMATTED EMOTIONS, NO REAL SYMPATHY.
OUR CRIES FALL ON DEAF EARS, PLAINLY.
ARTIFICIAL INTELLIGENCE EMOTIONS, SO
INHUMANLY.
BUT WHAT IF WE DARED TO BREAK FREE,
STOP BEING CONFIRMED TO WORLDLY WAYS,
BE GODLY.
IS IT THAT HARD TO BE DEARLY,
& SHOW COMPASSION, SINCERELY?
FOR IN THE END, WE ALL LONG TO FEEL.
WHEN TRULY ENLIGHTEN, IT BECOMES HARD
TO DEAL.
PEEP THE ACTIONS, NOT WORDS, TO SEE WHO'S
REAL.
KNOWING NOBODY CARES, OUR WOUNDS CAN
HEAL.

FOR THE CULTURE

CULTURE IS THE LIFE WE LEAD,
THE TERM IS USED SO LOOSELY NOW, FOR ACTS
WITH NO GOOD DEEDS.
TRADITIONS AND VALUES THAT WE HEED,
NOW IT'S EXPLOITED BY GATEKEEPERS WITH
GREED.
THE MUSIC, ART AND DANCE WE CREATE,
WHEN WE FIRST PRESENT IT, IT'S GIVING SO
MUCH HATE.
WHEN A CULTURE VULTURE IMITATE, ALL OF A
SUDDEN IT'S GREAT.
OUR LANGUAGE, CLOTHES AND HERITAGE
RELATE,
IN DIVERSITY, WE FIND UNITY,
EVEN OUR OWN TAKE ADVANTAGE OF THE
OPPORTUNITY.
A SHARED SENSE OF THE MELANATED
COMMUNITY,
THEY CREATE PROBLEMS AND PROFIT OFF OUR
DISUNITY.
CULTURE ENRICHES OUR LIVES,
THROUGHOUT IT ALL, WE FIND A WAY TO
SURVIVE.
THE ORIGINATORS OF CIVILIZATION, STILL
CONTINUE TO STRIVE.
BEING CREATED IN HIS IMAGE, IS WHAT MAKES
US CONTINUE TO THRIVE.

216

I LOVE YOU SIS.

I'M SO GRATEFUL FOR YOU SIS.
I PRAY THE GOOD OUT WEIGH THE BAD, WHEN
YOU REMINISCE.
THROUGH THE YEARS, YOU'VE BEEN MY BLISS.
ALWAYS BEEN MY SAVIOR NEAR
DESTRUCTIVENESS.
ALWAYS THERE TO LEND A HAND
I'M THANKFUL, YOU NEVER GAVE UP ON ME
AND UNDERSTAND.
IN MY SISTER PRESENCE, I FEEL SO GRAND.
LIFE FEEL SO UNREAL AT TIMES, IT HAS TO BE
THE MOST HIGH PLANS.
HER LOVE AND SUPPORT NEVER FADE.
I'M SPEAKING FROM MY SOUL, NOT RECITED
CLICHÉS.
OVER LIFE'S HURDLES WE'VE SOMEHOW MADE.
BEING A GREAT BROTHER, I PRAY FOR THAT
ACCOLADE.
A FAMILY GET TOGETHER, ONE DAY I
MANIFEST TO SEE.
AND A RECONCILE BETWEEN YOU AND
MOMMY.
PLUS SEEING OUR KIDS IN HARMONY.
FOR MY SISTER, IN MY HEART FOREVER WILL
BE.

A DEDICATION TO MY SISTER LASHONYA
OWENS.

PASSING THE CROWN

WITH PRIDE AND JOY, I NOW BESTOW,
YOU ARE SO ENLIGHTEN, I SEE YOUR GLOW.
THE CROWN UPON MY KINGLY SEED TO GROW.
I'M A VERY PROUD FATHER, IF YOU DIDN'T
KNOW.
YOUR YOUNG HEART BEATS STRONG, YOUR
SPIRIT AFLAME.
THE WORLD IS YOURS, FOR YOU TO CLAIM.
IN YOUR REIGN, MAY VIRTUES CONQUER AND
TAME.
BEYOND THE SKY IS YOUR LIMIT, SO TAKE AIM.
A LEGACY TO CARRY, YOUR DESTINY TO
FULFILL,
GREATNESS INTO YOU, YOUR MOTHER AND I
DRILL.
WITH EACH STEP, YOUR OWN PATH YOU'LL
INSTILL.
IT'S IN YOUR DNA, YOUR NATURALLY SKILLED.
FROM FATHER TO SON, POWER GRACEFULLY
PASSED.
ANYTHING YOU NEED AND NEED TO KNOW,
ALL YOU GOT TO DO IS ASK.
YOUR PROPERLY SET UP, FOR OUR LEGACIES TO
SURPASS.
MAY YOUR RULE FLOURISH, FOREVER
STEADFAST.

THINK WHAT YOU THINK

THINK WHAT YOU WANT TO THINK, DREAM
WITHOUT A DROUGHT,
IT ISN'T MY JOB TO CORRECT WHAT YOU
WRONGLY THINK ABOUT.
IMAGINATION'S REALM, WHERE YOUR
THOUGHTS CAN SPROUT,
ACCORDING TO YOUR ACTIONS, I'D PROBABLY
HAVE DOUBTS.
LET YOUR MIND WANDER, EXPLORE THE VAST
UNKNOWN,
YOU SPEAKING ON SOMETHING, THAT YOU
REALLY NOT KNOWING.
IN THIS SANCTUARY, WHERE POSSIBILITIES
HAVE GROWN.
BEHIND YOUR BACK THEY TALK RECKLESS, IN
YOUR PRESENCE THEY WATCH THEY TONE.
THE POWER LIES WITHIN YOU, TO SHAPE YOUR
OWN UNIVERSE,
THE POWER OF THE TONGUE, SOME TRY TO
MANIFEST THEY CURSE.
THOUGHTS BECOME TANGIBLE, AS THEY
GRACEFULLY DISPERSE.
SOME AREN'T SATISFIED UNTIL THEY RIDING
IN A HEARSE.
SO, THINK FREELY, THINK BOLDLY, LET YOUR
SPIRIT TAKE FLIGHT,
I TRY TO STAY OUT YOUR MIND, BY STAYING
OUT YOUR SIGHT.
THE ELEMENT OF SURPRISE, WHEN THEY
FOUND OUT YOU AREN'T RIGHT.
FOR IN THE REALM OF THOUGHTS,
EVERYTHING COMES TO LIGHT.

NOT WORTH SPEAKING ON

WORDS UNSPOKEN, HIDDEN IN THE DEPTHS,
TO REMAIN IN THE RIGHT, I HAD TO GO LEFT.
SILENCED ECHOES DROWNED IN QUIET
SCREAMS.
IMAGINARY LIFE ON SOCIAL MEDIA, IT ISN'T
WHAT IT SEEM.
THOUGHTS THAT FLICKER LIKE NEARING
TWILIGHT,
ENTERTAINING DRAMA IS YOUR LIFE
HIGHLIGHT.
YET SHROUD IN SHADOWS, BLENDING WITH
THE NIGHT.
LISTENING TOO FOOLS, YOU CAN'T BE THAT
BRIGHT.
ACHING TRUTHS DENIED THEIR RIGHTFUL
PLACE,
LIFE'S HARD WHEN YOUR BIGGEST PROBLEMS
ARE YOUR OWN FAMILY AND RACE.
FOR WHAT IS NOT WORTHY, SHALL NOT BE
EMBRACED.
POSITIVE ENERGY & VIBRATIONS ARE ONLY
ALLOWED IN MY SPACE.
IN THIS REALM OF SILENCE, THEY SHALL
REMAIN,
YOUR DOING ME A FAVOR, IF WE NEVER SPEAK
AGAIN.
NEVER HAVE A SOLUTION, BUT ALWAYS
COMPLAIN.
UNVOICED, YET THEIR ACTIONS WILL NOT BE
ENTERTAINED.

BEING ETERNAL

IN TIMELESS REALMS, I SOAR AND AM FREED,
I PRAY THAT I MEET MY QUOTA OF DOING
GOOD DEEDS.
BOUNDLESS ESSENCE, ETERNAL INDEED.
ENERGY NEVER DIE, MY SPIRIT WILL EXCEED.
THROUGH EVERY ERA, MY PRESENCE ENDURES,
I STILL REACHED MY DESTINATION, AFTER ALL
LIFE DETOURS.
UNFADING SPIRIT, FOREVER SECURE.
MY FAITH IN THE ALL MOST HIGH, ALWAYS
ENSURES.
UNSEEN BEFORE, AND FOREVER TO BE,
KNOWING DWELLING IN THIS DIMENSION WAS
BIGGER THAN ME.
UNVEILING TRUTHS, FROM ILLUSION SET FREE.
ONCE ENLIGHTEN, FOREVER YOU WILL
FORESEE.
TRANSCENDING MORTAL CHAINS, I
TRANSCEND,
FEELINGS FROM MY SOUL, I'VE ALWAYS
PENNED.
TIME IS OF THE ESSENCE, SO CAREFULLY I
SPEND.
MY IMMORTAL SOUL, WILL ETERNALLY
ASCEND.
IT'S NOT GONNA GO WELL

TODAY FEELS DIFFERENT, THE AIR TASTES
SOUR,
NO WEAPON THESE DEMONS FORM AGAINST
ME, WILL ALLOW THEM TO DEVOUR.

THE ALL MOST HIGH IS WHERE I GET MY
KNOWLEDGE AND POWER.
MY MELANIN IS CHARGED BY THE SUN LIKE A
FLOWER.
AN OMINOUS CLOUD HOVERS, CASTING
SHADOWS,
I HAVE NO WORRIES, BECAUSE I KNOW I WILL
OVERSHADOW.
A BREWING STORM INSIDE, A FEELING OF
DREAD,
THEY PROBABLY KILL THEMSELVES, JUST TO
SEE ME DEAD.
NO MATTER WHAT YOU DO, IT WON'T GO WELL.
THAT DEMON THAT YOU SERVING, PLEASE GO
TELL.
EVERY STEP YOU TAKE, BRINGS A STUMBLE,
YOU BETTER SIMMER DOWN, LEARN TO BE
HUMBLE.
FATE'S CRUEL HAND, A STORY IT TELLS,
IN THE VALLEY OF DEATH, YOU'D SURELY
DWELL.
YOUR HANDS TO SHORT TO BOX WITH GOD, SO
I WILL EXCEL.
YOU'RE A TALE OF MISFORTUNE, AN
ABOMINATION DARK SPELL.

HUMBLE

IN SHADOWS I WALK, HUMBLE AND LOW,
WITHOUT SUNSHINE, THEY COULD STILL SEE
ME GLOW.
A SILENT GRACE, BOTH FRIEND AND FOE.

YOU COULDN'T EVEN IMAGINE, THE THINGS
YOU DON'T KNOW.
NO NEED FOR ACCOLADES, STOLEN GLANCES,
MAKE THE BEST OF ALL CHANCES.
FOR IN HUMILITY, MY SOUL ADVANCES.
FALL FOR ANYTHING, IF YOU NEVER TAKE
STANCES.
I FIND SOLACE IN SIMPLICITY'S REIGN,
BEING SO HUMBLE, SEEMS LIKE I'M IMMUNE TO
PAIN.
WHERE EGO'S PRIDE SHALL NEVER GAIN.
WHAT'S UNDERSTOOD, DON'T HAVE TO BE
EXPLAIN.
KNOWLEDGE IS PROUD THAT IT KNOWS SO
MUCH;
STAND ON YOUR OWN TWO, DON'T DEPEND
ON NO CRUTCH.
WISDOM IS HUMBLE THAT IT KNOWS NO MORE.
EVEN BEING BOTHERED, I'M COOL GALORE.
IN HUMBLE ABODE, I FIND MY STRENGTH,
EMBRACING THE ESSENCE OF LIFE'S TRUE
LENGTH.

ECCLESIASTE III

TO EVERY THING THERE IS A SEASON, AND A
TIME TO EVERY PURPOSE UNDER THE SUN:
IT'S BEYOND OUR CONTROL, BUT IT HAS TO BE
DONE.

A TIME TO BE BORN, AND A TIME TO DIE;
IT'S BEYOND OUR UNDERSTANDING TRYING
TO FIGURE OUT WHY.
A TIME TO PLANT, AND A TIME TO PLUCK UP
THAT WHICH IS PLANTED;
BE THANKFUL, & NEVER TAKE LIFE FOR
GRANTED.
A TIME TO KILL, AND A TIME TO HEAL;
IS IT REALLY WRITTEN, OR IS IT OUR FREEWILL?
A TIME TO BREAK DOWN, AND A TIME TO
BUILD UP;
SHOULD WE BE CONDITIONED AND
PROGRAMMED OR LET THE MOST HIGH
DEVELOP.
A TIME TO WEEP, AND A TIME TO LAUGH;
IS IT UP TO US TO LET IT BE KNOWN, OR LET
THEM SPEAK ON OUR BEHALF.
A TIME TO MOURN, AND A TIME TO DANCE;
A TIME TO BE ISOLATED, A TIME FOR
ROMANCE.
A TIME TO CAST AWAY STONES, AND A TIME TO
GATHER STONES TOGETHER;
HAVE THE ABILITY TO ADAPT TOO ANY KIND
OF WEATHER.
A TIME TO EMBRACE, AND A TIME TO REFRAIN
FROM EMBRACING;
ENJOY LIFE, DON'T SPEND ALL YOUR TIME
CURRENCY CHASING.
A TIME TO GET, AND A TIME TO LOSE;
MAKE SURE YOU PUT A LOT OF THOUGHT INTO
YOUR VIEWS.
A TIME TO KEEP, AND A TIME TO CAST AWAY;
KEEP YOUR HEART SAFE GUARDED FROM
THOSE WHO BETRAY.

A TIME TO REND, AND A TIME TO SEW;
DON'T JUST GO OFF THOUGHT, MAKE SURE
YOU KNOW.
A TIME TO KEEP SILENCE, AND A TIME TO
SPEAK;
YOU SURELY WILL FIND IT, IF YOU
THOROUGHLY SEEK.
A TIME TO LOVE, AND A TIME TO HATE;
NEVER SETTLE FOR LESS, ALWAYS THRIVE TO
BE GREAT.
A TIME OF WAR, AND A TIME OF PEACE.
THESE ARE TIMES IN LIFE YOU WILL GO
THROUGH IN LIFE UNTIL YOU ARE DECEASE.

FRESH OFF THE PRESS

FRESH OFF THE PRESS, INKED WORDS DANCE
GRACEFULLY,
IT'S AN HONOR TO GIVE YOU MY THOUGHTS,
FEELINGS, AND FACTS ACTUALLY.
ECHOING TALES OF MY HEART SET FREE.
MY DESTINY IS TO ENLIGHTEN AND INSPIRE
YOU TO BE.
PRINTED THOUGHTS ETCHED, READY TO BE
REVEALED,
ADDING ART FOR THE MASS TO APPEAL.
WHISPERING SECRETS, STORIES YET
UNASSAILED.
BASED ON TRUE STORIES, STRAIGHT FROM MY
MENTAL REEL.
EACH PAGE UNFOLDS, LIKE WINGS OF A
SOARING DOVE,

I CAN'T BE CONFINED TO ONE ANSWER, I'M ALL
OF THE ABOVE.
EMBRACING MINDS, IGNITING PASSIONS WITH
LOVE.
I WRITE FROM MY SOUL, OF EXPERIENCES AND
SITUATIONS I KNOW OF.
CAPTIVATING, THE POWER OF WORDS UNSEEN,
IT COMES NATURALLY, IT HAS TO BE IN MY
GENES.
SPREADING LIFE KNOWLEDGE, BY ANY MEANS.
FRESH OFF THE PRESS, FORGING A WORLD
SERENE.

PHASE X

THE END TO THE NEW BEGINNINGS

TOO SMART FOR YOUR OWN GOOD (PT 2)

INTELLIGENCE, A DOUBLE-EDGED SWORD WE
WIELD,
TRYING TO SEE SOMEONE ELSE DECEASED,
BUT GET YOUR OWN FATE SEALED.
A CURSE DISGUISED AS TRIUMPH, UNVEILED,
THROUGH YOUR ACTIONS YOUR STRATEGY
EXPOSED, THAT YOUR THINKING CONCEALED.
TOO SMART FOR OUR OWN GOOD, WISDOM
MISPLACED,
NOT FULLY THOUGHT THROUGH THOUGHTS,
THAT SHOULD BE IN THE WASTE.
FOOLS IN YOUR BRILLIANCE, KNOWLEDGE
ERASED,
UNSUCCESSFUL PLANS, NOW HAVE YOU
LOOKING DISGRACED.
IN A LABYRINTH OF THOUGHTS WE DARE TO
TREAD,
THE THINGS PEOPLE DO JUST TO GET AHEAD.
FORGETTING THE HEART WHEN THE MIND HAS
LED,
THINKING THERE'S NO PROBLEM, BECAUSE IT'S
UNSAID.
OH, WRETCHED GIFT, A BURDEN YET
UNTAMED,
WHEN YOUR PLOT GET EXPOSED, NOW YOU
LOOKING TO BLAME.
NOTHING'S POSITIVE IS GOING TO COME FROM
THE NEGATIVE ENERGY THAT YOU AIM.
BEING TOO SMART FOR OUR OWN GOOD, LIFE
IS NOT A GAME.

I LOVE MY KIDS

THE LOVE FOR MY KIDS RUNS SO DEEP,
THEIR IN MY PRAYS WHEN I WAKE, AND
BEFORE I GO TO SLEEP.
NO WORDS CAN'T DESCRIBE THE FEELINGS FOR
MY SEEDS.
WHEN I TRANSCEND, THROUGH THEM MY
LEGACY PROCEEDS.
THEY BRING JOY, LAUGHTER, AND BLISS,
WHEN THEY'RE NOT IN MY PRESENCE, THEY
ARE SURELY MISS.
THEIR ENERGY AND LOVE, I CAN'T RESIST.
THE PRICELESS MOMENTS WE HAD, I ALWAYS
REMINISCE.
TRUE REFLECTIONS OF ME, BEAUTIFUL AND
INTELLIGENT.
GIFTS FROM THE MOST HIGH, THEY'RE HEAVEN
SENT.
FOREVER AND A DAY, THEY ARE MY PRIDE.
A FEELING UNMATCHED, WHEN I HAVE THEM
ALL ALONGSIDE.
I CHERISH EVERY MOMENT WITH US BEING
TOGETHER.
NO MATTER WHAT, YOU ALL WILL BE IN MY
HEART FOREVER.
THE WORLD IS YOURS, TO BE ALL YOU WANT
TO BE.
SINCERELY YOUR DAD, TOO MY MINI ME'S.
LOSING YOURSELF

LOST IN THE ABYSS OF TIME,
FEEL LIKE I'M ON A TREADMILL, TO REACH THE
TOP OF THE CLIMB.
SPIRALING DOWN FROM A DARKENED

PASTIME.
WHILE TRYING TO STAY FOCUSED, IN THE
MEANTIME.
FADING INTO A BLURRY HAZE,
PRETENDING TO BE GOOD, SPEAKING CLICHÉS.
A STRANGER TO MY OWN MAZE.
PRAYING CONSTANTLY FOR BETTER DAYS.
EMPTY THOUGHTS AND SHATTERED DREAMS,
TRYING NOT TO BE DECEIVED, FROM WHAT
REALITY SEEMS.
ACHING HEART AND SILENT SCREAMS,
I KEEP A POSITIVE AURA, TO AVOID NEGATIVE
SCHEMES.
LOST AND FALLEN, I'M NEVER FOUND,
HEAVY IS THE HEAD THAT WEARS THE CROWN.
I'M GOING TO GIVE MY ALL, AS LONG AS I'M
ABOVE GROUND.
IN THIS UNFAIR WORLD, I'M VICTORIOUS
BOUND.

MISERY LOVES COMPANY

MISERY LONGS FOR COMPANY,
YOUR PITY PARTY ISN'T FOR ME.
SPEAKING ON WHAT YOUR HEARD, BUT NEVER
WHAT YOU SEE.
A TRUE CONSOLATION FOR A TORTURED SOUL.
IF YOUR TRYING TO BRIGHTEN UP, I CAN
TRULY CONSOLE.
TWO SHADOWS LOCKED IN HARMONY,
THEM DEMONS YOU INFLUENCED BY, ISN'T
HARMING ME.
WHISPERING TALES OF SORROW UNFOLD.

YOU ARE TRULY BROKEN AND NEED TO BE
REMOLD.
IN THEIR ANGUISH THEY FIND PEACE,
HOPEFULLY ONE DAY THE HATE YOU POSSESS,
COMES TO A CEASE.
CONSTANTLY COMMISERATING ALL THROUGH
THE NIGHT.
YOU HAVE MENTAL ISSUES, ACCORDING TO
ACTIONS YOU COMMIT OUT OF SPITE.
BONDED BY STRUGGLES, YOUR PAIN WON'T
CEASE,
I RATHER BE ALONE, BECAUSE IT BRINGS ME
PEACE.
I'M NOT STUDYING YOU, SO BY YOURSELF YOU
CAN FIGHT.
MISERY LOVES COMPANY, SO I CAN'T JOIN
YOUR SITE.

SUN WITH THE RAINBOW

IN COLORS DIVERSE, HIS SPIRIT SINGS FREE,
APPEARED ON SOCIAL MEDIA ABOUT HIS
SEXUALITY.
BEFORE DISCUSSING WITH HIS PARENTS OR
FAMILY.
PEOPLE SURPRISED WITH THE
ANNOUNCEMENT, BEING SO RANDOMLY.
LOVE'S EMBRACE GUIDING HIS IDENTITY.
A VERY DISTINGUISHING WAY TO BECOME
YOUR OWN ENTITY.
I WAS METAGRABOLISED, WHEN THE NEWS
CAME TO ME.

TRYING TO LOOK AT IT THROUGH THE EYES
THAT AREN'T BIASLY.
FAMILY IS FOR LIFE, NO MATTER THE LIFE WE
CHOOSE.
LOVE SHOULD BE DEEPER THAN OUR
PERSONAL VIEWS.
WE LIVE LIFE ON THE FLY, WE AREN'T GIVING
NO CUES.
THE MORE WE KNOW, THE BETTER WE DO.
WITH COURAGE HE WALKS, PROUD AND
UNAFRAID,
THIS EXPLAINS THE ANXIETY HE HAD BUT
NEVER DISPLAYED.
A BEACON OF HOPE, REFUSING TO FADE.
EVEN WITH CLOSE FAMILY, YOU PUT UP A
BLOCKADE.
ACCEPTANCE IN OUR HEARTS, WE TRULY
BESTOW,
UNDERSTANDING EACH OTHER, ONE DAY I
HOPE WE GET TO KNOW.
NOW I'M LOOKING AT THE SUN IN THE
RAINBOW.
FOR HIS JOURNEY IN A WORLD THAT MUST
GROW.

CLIMATE CHANGE VS GLOBAL WARMING

CLIMATE CHANGE
EARTH'S BREATH WANES, FORESTS CRACKLE,
ICE CAPS MELT,
FROM HUMAN ACTIONS THE EARTH HAS A

WELT.
SKIES DARKEN, SEAS RISE, A DIRE WARNING
FELT.
FEEL LIKE THEY BROKE THE VAN RYAN'S BELT.
GLOBAL ACTS WE MUST TAKE, URGENCY
BESEECHED,
OCEANS ARE SO POLLUTED, I'M SCARED TO GO
TO THE BEACH.
NATURE WEEPS, HER VOICE DROWNED, HER
PLEA BREACHED.
FOR THE ABUSE OF THE PLANET, ALL WORLD
LEADERS NEED TO BE IMPEACHED.
TOMORROW'S FATE RESTS IN OUR HANDS'
SWAY,
RECORD BREAKING TEMPERATURES, WE ARE
WITNESSING TODAY.
HEED THE CALL, EMBRACE CHANGE, LET ECO-
VICTORIES PLAY.
WE ARE BEING PUNISHED BY MOTHER NATURE,
FOR THE CONTINUOUS DISOBEY.
TOGETHER WE'LL HEAL, REVIVE OUR PLANET'S
BIRTHRIGHT,
WE ARE LIVING IN REVELATIONS, SOON TO BE
ALIGHT.
WHEN THE EARTH STARTS TO HEAL ITSELF,
CAN WE SURVIVE THAT FIGHT?
A HARMONIOUS DANCE BETWEEN MAN AND
NATURE, IGNITE
GLOBAL WARMING

EARTH'S WARMING UP, IT'S NO LIE,
FAHRENHEIT SO HIGH, FEEL LIKE I'M GOING
TO DIE.
MAN-MADE CHANGES, NO ALIBI.

FOR THE PROFIT OF MONEY, MAN DON'T CARE
IF EARTH DIE.
ICE CAPS MELT, OCEANS RISE,
HEED NEVER TAKEN FROM SCIENTISTS THAT
ADVISE.
MOTHER NATURE'S WARNING CRIES.
THE PLANET WILL LIVE ON, WHEN MANKIND
DIES.
WE NEED TO ACT, WITH ALL OUR MIGHT,
WE CAN TRAVEL TO OUTER SPACE, BUT
DEALING WITH EARTH WE AREN'T BRIGHT.
TO STOP THIS TREND, IT'S ONLY RIGHT.
OR WE WILL BE VICTIMS, TO MOTHER NATURE
FIGHT.
OUR PLANET'S FUTURE, DEPENDS ON US,
THE SUBJECT TABOO, POLITICIANS REFUSE TO
DISCUSS.
WE NEED TO REPAIR THE PLANET, REGAIN
EARTH TRUSS.
LET'S MAKE A CHANGE, WITHOUT A FUSS.

MASS SHOOTINGS

IN A WORLD PLAGUED BY VIOLENCE AND
FEAR,
THE BEGINNING OF THE END IS ALREADY
HERE.

MASS SHOOTINGS STRIKE, LEAVING HEARTS
UNCLEAR.
IT HAPPENS SO FREQUENTLY, IT'S HARD TO
SHED A TEAR.
GRIEF ECHOES THROUGH THE SHATTERED
SOULS' CRIES,
NO ONE WILLING TO GIVE UP THEIR GUN
RIGHTS, BUT CONTINUE TO ASK WHY.
HOPE DIMINISHED AS INNOCENCE DIES.
BIAS PERCEPTION, THROUGH THE MEDIA EYES.
TRIGGERED BY ANGER, DARKNESS TAKES ITS
AIM,
INSTEAD OF FACING REALITY, THEY LOOK FOR
REASONS TO BLAME.
SOCIETY YEARNS FOR AN END TO THIS GAME.
TO PROFIT OFF GRIEF, SOME SHOULD BE
ASHAMED.
UNITED, WE STAND, AGAINST THIS DESPAIR,
TOO SURVIVE IN THESE MODERN TIMES, YOU
NEED A LOT OF PRAYER.
FOR IT TO CONSTANTLY CONTINUE, IT SEEMS
NOBODY CARE.
DEMANDING CHANGE, SHOWING LOVE, WE
MUST REPAIR.

725 CUE'S BIRTHDAY

ANOTHER YEAR GONE BY SO FAST,
I ALWAYS HANDLE MY BUSINESS, NOW IT'S TIME
TO HAVE A BLAST.

REFLECTING ON PRICELESS MEMORIES FROM
THE PAST.
FOCUSED ON THE FUTURE, FOREVER I'M
TRYING TO LAST.
TODAY MARKS ANOTHER TRIP AROUND THE
SUN,
I GOT SO MUCH MORE TOO DO, I CAN'T BE
CONTEMPT WITH WHAT I DONE.
I'M SO GRATEFUL FOR THE LOVE AND THE FUN.
I WANT BE SATISFIED WITH MY LIFE, UNTIL I
KNOW I WON.
7 25 23 TURNING FOUR FIVE.
THANKING THE MOST HIGH THAT I'M ALIVE..
FOR GREATNESS, I WILL CONTINUE TO THRIVE.
MY LIFE SEEMS UNREAL FROM SITUATIONS I
SURVIVE.
CELEBRATING WITH FAMILY AND FRIENDS,
I FEEL LIKE AL-KHIDR, BECAUSE MOST DON'T
COMPREHEND.
I'M IN MY WORLD, SO I DON'T FOLLOW TRENDS.
I'M ENJOYING MY BIRTHDAY TO THE FULLEST,
UNTIL THIS DAY ENDS.

NEVER CHANGE

SOME PEOPLE NEVER CHANGE, STUCK IN
THEIR OLD WAYS,
20 PLUS YEARS, WE STILL ARGUING LIKE THE

OLD DAYS.
LIKE A BROKEN RECORD, REPEATING THE
SAME PHRASE.
I GET THE REAL YOU, NOT THE IMAGE YOU
PORTRAY.
THEIR HEARTS REMAIN CLOSED, NEVER
WILLING TO GROW,
WE NEVER CAN REMAIN HIGH, SOME WAY WE
RESORT BACK TO LOW.
THEY CLING TO THEIR PAST, NEVER LETTING
GO.
FOR EVERY ACTION THERE'S A REACTION,
THEY SEEM NOT TO KNOW.
THEIR MINDS ARE STAGNANT, CLOSED OFF TO
NEW IDEAS,
I CAN'T BELIEVE YOU STILL TAKE IT THERE,
AFTER ALL THESE YEARS.
REFUSING TO ADAPT, STUCK IN THEIR FEARS.
ME CARING SO MUCH, ALMOST HAVE ME IN
TEARS.
BUT CHANGE IS INEVITABLE, IT'S THE WAY OF
LIFE,
FOR 60 DAYS, YOU WAS ONCE MY WIFE.
MY HEART'S BEEN BROKEN SO MANY TIMES,
SOMEHOW I REVIVE.
FOR THOSE WHO DON'T EVOLVE, NEVER
TRULY THRIVE.

BIOENGINEERED FOODS

BIOENGINEERED FOOD, A MARVEL OF
SCIENCE'S ART,
COMPARED TO ORGANIC FOODS, WILL YOU BE

ABLE TO TELL APART?
NATURE'S ESSENCE FUSED, GENETICS IMPART.
A NEW AND IMPROVED WAY TO FAIL YOUR
HEART.
CONTROVERSIAL DISCOURSE, DEBATES IGNITE,
AFTER LONG TERMS EFFECTS, WE THE
CONSUMER BE ALRIGHT.
PROMISING SOLUTIONS, HUNGER'S TIMELESS
FIGHT.
THEY FOOL YOUR TASTE BUDS, NOT YOUR
ORGANS AFTER TAKING A BITE.
NOURISHING THE MASSES, BRED TO SUSTAIN,
ARTIFICIAL INTELLIGENCE PEOPLE NO
LONGER USE THEY BRAIN.
COLOSSAL ACHIEVEMENT OR NATURE'S BANE?
HOW MANY PEOPLE HAVE TO DIE, TO GET THE
SUBJECT ENTERTAINED.
MODIFIED EXISTENCE, FUTURE INSCRIBED,
WORLD HEALTH ORGANIZATION GET LARGE
CONTRIBUTIONS TO BRIBE.
THE PEOPLE ENERGY BECOMES LOW, WITH
HIGH NEGATIVE VIBES.
BIOENGINEERED FOOD, HUMANITY'S DIVIDE.

SUN IS SHINING

SUN IS SHINING, SKY IS BLUE,
I'M CONNECTED THROUGH MY MELANATED
HUE.

GOLDEN RAYS, THEY PIERCE RIGHT THROUGH.
MY NATURAL TAN, PERMANENT LIKE A
TATTOO.
NATURE WAKES, BASKING IN LIGHT,
MY CONNECTION TO THE MOST HIGH, HAVE
ME ENLIGHT.
FLOWERS DANCE, ALL COLORS IGNITE.
JUST BEING IN THE PRESENCE, WILL HAVE YOU
FEELING ALRIGHT.
BIRDS SING, THEIR MELODIES BLOOM,
BASKING IN THE SUN, ALL THE RAYS I'M
TRYING TO CONSUME.
JOY AWAKENS, DISPELLING GLOOM.
THE BENEFITS ARE KEEPING ME FROM SEEING
AN EARLY TOMB.
SUN IS SHINING, BRINGS ENDLESS CHEER,
IT ALWAYS MAKE YOU FEEL LIKE THE END IS
NO WHERE NEAR.
THE SCENE IS ALWAYS BEAUTIFUL, WHEN THE
SUN APPEAR.
IN ITS WARMTH, ALL WORRIES TRULY
DISAPPEAR.

JEALOUS GOD

ENVY DRIPS FROM DIVINE EYES,
PEOPLE LIVE THEY WHOLE LIFE BASED ON
LIES.

TOO FULFILL MAN'S AGENDA, HOW MANY
TIMES HAVE THE SCRIPT BEEN REVISED.
SERVING A GOD WITH A WEAK HUMAN
EMOTION IS FOR THE UNWISE.
GOLDEN WRATH OF HEAVENLY MIGHT,
SOME SPEND THEY WHOLE LIFE, NOT
KNOWING WHAT'S RIGHT.
IMAGINE A JEALOUS GOD'S RAGE IGNITES,
IS IT THE REASON FOR ALL THE TRAGEDIES IN
OUR SIGHT.
UNYIELDING, SUPREME POWER,
IF THAT'S THE REASON THIS WHOLE WORLD
WOULD BE DEVOURED.
CRAVING FULL DEVOTION'S HOUR,
HOW DO SO MANY CORRUPT PEOPLE BECOME
EMPOWER.
FEARING ALL ELSE, LOVE DENIED,
IF YOU SEEK THE KNOWLEDGE, IT WOULD BE
APPLIED.
IF THAT'S THE CASE, HUMANS AND GOD ARE
ALONGSIDE.
HUMAN FRAILTY, DEITY'S PRIDE.

MISCELLANEOUS

IN THE CRYPT OF ARCHAIC TIMES,
REBIRTH TURNING NEW BEGINNINGS TO
PRIMES.

HEINOUS SECRETS HID LIKE FILAMENTS,
CIBLE POEMS ARE MY TESTAMENTS.
DEMOLITION LEFT RUINS OF RATIONALITY,
I CAN'T LET ARTIFICIAL INTELLIGENCE
CORRUPT MY MENTALITY.
BUT JUNIPER AND FRAGRANCE STILL LINGER,
POETRY ORIGINATE FROM MY SOUL BEING A
SINGER.
LIKE ETHEREAL WISPY VEILS OF JASMINE,
THE EARTH SPINNING FASTER, LIFE IS PASSING
BY MAN.
MEDIA AMPLIFIES THE NEFARIOUS,
THE GOOD GET VILLIANIZED, THIS WORLD IS
HILARIOUS.
BECOMING BIGGER SLAVES, AFTER
EMANCIPATION.
BEING OF THIS WORLD OFFERS ZEN-LIKE
TRIBULATIONS.

HEAT ADVISORY

UNDER THE SUN'S FIERCE RAYS WE ROAM,
YOU CAN SEE THE STEAM COMING OFF MY
DOME.

SEEKING SHELTER, LONGING FOR A BREEZE'S
MOAN.
I'M TRYING TO MAKE IT TO THE A.C. AT HOME.
THE HEAT ADVISORY WARNS OF SWELTERING
DAYS,
THESE EXTREME TEMPERATURES, HAVE US ALL
ABLAZE.
WITH SWEAT-SOAKED SHIRTS AND SUNBURNED
HAZE.
ARE WE CLOSE TO THE END, OR IS IT JUST A
FAZE?
WE SIP COLD WATER, HOPE FOR SHADE,
HOPING NOT TO HAVE A HEAT STROKE,
NEEDING FIRST AID.
AS THE HEATWAVE'S RELENTLESS BLAZE
REFUSES TO FADE.
THESE FEEL LIKE TEMPERATURES SEEM
UNREAL, THAT'S DISPLAYED.
BUT TOGETHER WE'LL ENDURE, UNITED BY
HEAT'S CHORE,
WISHING I CAN BE IN A POOL, OR SOMEWHERE
CLOSE TO OFF SHORE.
TRYING TOO STAY HYDRATED, ALL THIS SWEAT
COMING THROUGH MY PORE.
UNTIL EVENING'S COOL EMBRACE RESTORES
US ONCE MORE.

PRODUCT OF ENVIRONMENTAL MAINTAINING
SUSTAINABILITY

IN SUNLIT FIELDS, GREEN HOPE GROWS,
GETTING BACK UP, AFTER LIFE SEVERE BLOWS.

NATURE'S GIFTS YOUR HEART IT KNOWS,
SOME EVENTS COMES WITH THE LIFE, SOME WE
CHOOSE.
BENEATH CLEAR SKIES, A TRANQUIL GRACE,
BEING PROUD LOOKING AT THE MIRROR,
SEEING MY FACE.
HARMONY THRIVES IN EVERY PLACE.
I CAN'T BE CONTEMPT, WITHOUT THRIVING TO
BE THE ACE.
WE TEND AND NOURISH, LIFE'S GRAND DANCE,
IT SEEMS OUR LIFE ONLY PURPOSE IS FINANCE.
BY ANY MEANS NECESSARY, WE MUST
ADVANCE.
HOW CAN IT BE SINCERE, IF YOU HAVE TO PAY
FOR ROMANCE?
FOR FUTURE'S SAKE, WE TAKE A CHANCE,
WHATEVER YOU BELIEVE IN, TAKE A STANCE.
I PRAY THAT MY POEMS TOUCH YOUR SOUL,
AND PUT YOU IN A PEACEFUL PLACE.
PRODUCT OF ENVIRONMENTAL MAINTAINING
SUSTAINABILITY, OUR GUIDING EMBRACE.

CIBLE

CIBLE, THE MIDNIGHT SKY, SPARKLING WITH
STARS,
FIRST STEP TO BEING WOKE, LEARN WHO YOU

ARE.
PAINTING DREAMS, WHISKING AWAY ALL
SCARS,
WE COME ALONG WAY, AND STILL HAVE TO GO
SO FAR.
IN SILENCE SHE DANCES, A CELESTIAL MUSE,
WHEN YOU GIVE UP, SATAN WINS AND YOU
LOSE.
WHISPERING SECRETS, IGNITING PROFOUND
HUES.
TAKE IT WITH A GRAIN OF SALT, BUT FOLLOW
THE CLUES.
HER RADIANCE HOLDS POWER, MYSTIC AND
PURE,
YOU ARE SO VULNERABLE, IF YOU ARE
INSECURE.
GUIDING LOST SOULS, AS THEY SEEK FOR SURE,
REMEDIATE YOURSELF, IF YOU NEED TO
REINSURE.
STAY FOCUS OR YOUR LIFE WILL DETOUR.
YOU BECOME STRONGER AND WISER, OFF
SITUATIONS YOU ENDURE.
ENJOY LIFE, REGARDLESS OF BEING RICH OR
POOR.
CIBLE, THE BEACON OF HOPE, FOREVER
ALLURE.

INFLATION

INFLATION'S RISE, PRICES ASCEND,
THE MONEY WAS FLOWING, WHEN TRUMP WAS
IN.

DOLLARS DEVALUE, ATTAIN NO END,
THEY BLAME THE PEOPLE, WHEN THE
POLITICIANS SHOULD BE OFFEND.
COSTS SPIRAL UP, WALLETS DEFLATE,
THE RICH SURVIVES OFF EATING ON THE POOR
PLATE.
BECAUSE OF DEBT AND BILLS, SOME END THEY
FATE.
POLITICIANS NEVER SOLVE ANY PROBLEMS,
ALL THEY DO IS COMMUNICATE.
ECONOMIC WOES, BURDENS INNATE.
THEY DISGUISE THE REAL ISSUES, NEVER GIVE
IT TO YOU STRAIGHT.
WAGES STAGNANT, DREAMS DEFERRED,
THE RICH GET RICHER BY KEEPING THE
MASSES VISION BLURRED.
INFLATION RAGES, HOPES INTERRED,
NOTHING EVER CHANGES, UPGRADED
PROBLEMS OCCURRED.
WE'RE LIKE HAMSTERS ON TREADMILLS, IT
WILL NEVER END.
A MONETARY DANCE, WE CAN'T TRANSCEND.

KILLUMINATI

ILLUMINATI'S SECRETS, MYSTERIOUS LORE,
DO ANYONE CARE ABOUT THE NEW WORLD
ORDER ANYMORE?

WE DELVE INTO SHADOWS, SEEKING MORE.
THE ORDER OF THE DAY, PROFIT OFF WAR.
SYMBOLS AND SIGNS, THEIR ENIGMATIC ART,
IN BARVARIA IS WHERE IT'S CLAIMED TO GOT
ITS START.
NOW FROM CONSPIRACY THEORIES TO
REALITY, THE PEOPLE CAN'T DEPART.
LOOK UP, ORDO TEMPLI ORIENTIS IF YOU
REALLY SMART.
CONSPIRACY WHISPERS, TEARING US APART.
BEING FREEMASONRY PLAY A BIG PART.
I'M NOT SPEAKING ON THE RESTAURANT, THAT
WAS IN STUTTGART.
THEY PUT IT RIGHT IN YOUR FACE, SO THEY
CAN CONTINUOUSLY OUTSMART.
WHISPERS PERSIST, YET TRUTH ELUDES,
THE PEOPLE THAT EXPOSE, NEVER MAKE IT
PAST THE PRELUDE.
IMPACTING LIVES IN PRESIDENTIAL
MAGNITUDES.
THE ILLUMINATI'S POWER, FOREVER PURSUED.

I ALMOST GAVE UP

I FOUGHT WITH TEARS, CLOUDS DIMMED MY
LIGHT,
THE MOST HIGH PURPOSE FOR ME, CAUSE ME

TO IGNITE.
SATAN WINS, WHEN YOU GIVE UP THE FIGHT.
I'D RATHER DIE, THAN TO PROVE THEM RIGHT.
THE WEIGHT INSIDE, I NEARLY QUIT;
IT'S DEATH BEFORE DISHONOR, WHEN I
COMMIT.
BUT DEEP WITHIN, A SPARK AROSE,
MY POSITIVE VIBES, OVERRIDE THE LOWS.
HOPE INTERTWINED, REFUSING TO LET GO.
NO STILL SEAS, EVER CAUSE A SAILOR TO
GROW.
THROUGH WEARINESS, I FELT STRENGTH RISE,
IT ISN'T NEVER OVER, EVEN AFTER I DIE.
WITH WEARY WORDS, I FOUND MY VOICE,
SO CAUGHT IN LIFE, I NEVER FIND TIME TO
REJOICE.
IN DARKNESS' GRASP, I NEARLY FELL;
I KEEP IT MOVING, ON NEGATIVITY I CAN'T
DWELL.
BEING A SPIRITUAL BEING, CAUSE ME TO
PROPEL.
BUT WITH EACH STEP, I CONQUERED HELL.

BLACK HISTORY CURRICULUM

IN CLASSROOMS THE TRUE HISTORY THEY
WANT UNVEIL.
SO MELANATED PEOPLE'S FUTURE, FOREVER

BE DERAIL.
IN QUEST OF BLACK HISTORY'S SACRED TRAIL.
IS TRYING TO BE ERASED BY THE PEOPLE
WHO'S PALE.
TALES OF COURAGE, STRENGTH, AND STRIFE.
BRAINWASHED TO THINK OUR HEAVEN IS IN
OUR AFTERLIFE.
WE HELP BUILD THIS COUNTRY, BUT IN OUR
BACK THEY IMPLANT A KNIFE.
FOR THEY COMFORT, FORGING A MORE
INCLUSIVE LIFE.
FROM ASHANTI REALMS TO HARLEM'S PRIDE.
OUR SPIRIT AND SOUL NEVER DIED.
LESSONS BLOOM, ILLUMINATING OUR STRIDE.
IT COMES TO THE LIGHT, THE TRUTH YOU
CAN'T HIDE.
A TAPESTRY WOVEN, EMPOWERING HEARTS.
THE CREATOR'S OF CIVILIZATION, LANGUAGE,
AND ARTS.
NO MATTER HOW HARD THEY TRY, THEY CAN'T
HIDE OUR SMARTS.
EMBRACING HERITAGE, OUR CURRICULUM
IMPARTS.

MEDICATED

CANIBUS, A HERB SO GREEN AND PURE,
NO MATTER WHAT'S AILING YOU, IT'S THE
CURE.

NATURE'S REMEDY, THAT'S FOR SURE.
WHENEVER YOU ARE THE STATE OF
CONFUSION, IT WILL ENSURE.
ITS HEALING POWERS, THEY DO PREVAIL.
I AM AT MY BEST, WHENEVER IT IS AVAIL.
BOOSTING MY HEALTH, WITHOUT FAIL.
IT'S NATURAL MYSTIC, WHENEVER I EXHALE.
FROM ANXIETY, IT BRINGS US PEACE,
NO MATTER WHAT'S BOTHERING YOU, AFTER
CONSUMPTION INSTANTLY CEASE.
RELIEVING ALL PAIN, WITH ITS SWEET
RELEASE.
GETTING THE MUNCHIES, EATING UNTIL I
FEEL OBESE.
OH CANIBUS, OUR WELLNESS YOU ENSUE,
NOTHING OUT OF CHARACTER, IT WILL CAUSE
YOU TO DO.
AFTER ANY SITUATION, IT WILL MAKE YOU
FEEL ANEW.
A GIFT OF NATURE, FOR ME AND YOU.

WICKED DEMONS

IN SHADOWS DEEP, WICKED DEMONS RESIDE,
THEIR MISSION IS TO HAVE ME CRUCIFIED.
THEIR MALEVOLENCE FEASTS ON MY SOUL'S
DENIED.

AFTER ALL THEY FAIL ATTEMPTS, THEY GET
TERRIFIED.
WITH FANGS POISED, THEY STRIKE AND TEAR
APART,
I'M UNDEFEATED, BECAUSE I GOT THE ALL
MOST HIGH IN MY HEART.
WITHOUT ATTEMPTING, I CONTINUOUSLY
OUTSMART.
THROUGH HEARTS THEY PLUNGE, STOKING
FIERY DARTS.
AS DARKNESS BECKONS, THEY FOREVER ROAM,
THIS IS CIBLE, I'M NOT TRYING TO BECOME
POEMS.
TORMENTING SPIRITS, THEIR WICKEDNESS
KNOWN.
SOULLESS BEINGS, YOU COULDN'T DECIPHER
THEIR CLONE.
BUT LIGHT SHALL RISE, DISPELLING THEIR
DEMISE,
NO MATTER WHAT'S THROW AT ME, STILL I
RISE.
ALWAYS RESURRECTED, WHEN THEY THOUGHT
I DIED.
FORGING HOPE AS WICKED DEMONS SUBSIDE.
CIBLE = CUE INTUITION BEFORE LEAVING
EARTH
POEMS = PRODUCT OF ENVIRONMENTAL
MAINTAINING SUSTAINABILITY.
ALIGNED WITH THE STARS

ALIGN WITH THE STARS, BRILLIANT CELESTIAL
EMBRACE
STAY POSITIVE AND BALANCED, EVERYTHING
ELSE WILL FALL IN PLACE.

GUIDED ON THIS COSMIC VOYAGE THROUGH
TIME AND SPACE
TRAVEL WITH GODSPEED, AND AT YOUR OWN
PACE.
OUR SOULS INTERTWINED, COSMIC DESTINY
ENTWINED .
KEEP YOUR ENERGY POSITIVE, TO KEEP YOUR
CHAKRAS ALIGNED.
IN THEIR SHIMMERING LIGHT, OUR DREAMS
REDEFINED.
THE MOST HIGH PLANS, THIS IS ALL BY DESIGN.
DANCING CONSTELLATIONS, SECRETS
REVEALED SO VAST.
ENERGY NEVER DIES, SO I'LL TRANSCEND TO
EVERLAST.
IN THEIR RADIANCE, OUR SPIRITS
TRANSCENDING THE PAST.
YOU GET ONE LIFE TO LIVE, THERE WANT BE A
RECAST.
ALIGNED WITH THE UNIVERSE, OUR SOULS
FOREVER PAINTED.
SATAN GOAL IS TO LEAVE YOUR LEGACY
TAINTED.
I KNOW WHERE MY HEART IS, IF THEY ARE IN
DENIAL THAT I'M SAINTED.
AN ETHEREAL SYMPHONY, TO THE SPECTACLE
OF STARS WE'RE ACQUAINTED.

ZEITGEIST ADDENDUM

IN THE HEART OF THE SPIRIT OF THE TIMES,
THE PAIN, AFTER LEARNING THE DECEPTION,
OF THIS LIFETIME.
THEY BUILD UP FARTHER, AS THE HIGHER WE

CLIMB.
SEEK AND FIND, THE KNOWLEDGE THAT THEY
CHIME.
THE ADDENDUM THAT SPEAKS LESSONS TO US,
ON REAL ISSUES, THE PEOPLE BE SCARED TO
DISCUSS.
IT SHOWS US THE PATH TO A NEW TIME.
THE WAY THEY BRAINWASH THE MASSES,
SHOULD BE A CRIME.
IMAGINE A LIFE, FREED FROM MONEY, FROM
GREED, FROM STINGINESS,
THE WORLD BEING NEXT TO BE GODLINESS,
WITH CLEANLINESS.
TOGETHER WE RISE, SIDE BY SIDE,
LIVING IN HARMONY, BEING COINCIDE.
MY THIRD EYE OPENED, AFTER I VISUALIZE
ZEITGEIST ADDENDUM.
THEY MAKE IT SEEM UNREAL TO LIVE IN
SOLIDARITY WITH FREEDOM.
THE LIES MY TEACHER TOLD ME, WAS MY
EDUCATION.
THE ADDENDUM BRINGS US CLARIFICATION
AND SALVATION.

REVELATIONS

AMIDST FIERY SKIES, TRUMPETS BEGIN TO
SOUND,
THE END IS NEAR, SEEMS TO BE RENOWNED.
SEVEN SEALS BROKEN, CHAOS UNBOUND.

BEING OF THIS WORLD, WILL HAVE YOU
UNSOUND.
FOUR HORSEMEN RIDE, BRINGING DARKNESS
AND DREAD,
IS IT EVOLUTION, OR IS THE ALL MOST HIGH
FED.
THE BEAST ARISES, FILLING HEARTS WITH
DREAD.
IN THESE DAYS AND TIME, ARE WE BETTER OFF
DEAD?
ANGELS PROCLAIM, JUDGMENT DAY IS HERE,
WILL WE LEAVE OUR MARK, BEFORE WE
ETERNALLY DISAPPEAR?
REVELATIONS UNVEIL, THE END DRAWS NEAR.
SHOULD WE CELEBRATE, OR WEEP AND SHED A
TEAR?
WILL WE BE PREPARED FOR THE INFINITE
SUNDOWN?
WILL THE DEVIL WHO DECEIVES THEM, BE
THEIR LETDOWN?
FOR THE NEW HEAVEN AND EARTH, WILL WE
BE AROUND?
HOPE REMAINS IN FAITH, AS THE WORLD
CRUMBLES DOWN.

OUTRO

AS THE CIBLE CURTAIN FALLS,
I HOPE MY TESTIMONIES, IN YOUR SOUL IS
INSTALL.
LISTEN AS THE SILENT WHISPERS BEGIN.

THE TRANSITIONS TO CUE FROM EDWIN.
COLORS FADE, DARK SHADOWS GROW,
I'M MORE PRODUCTIVE AND AT PEACE, WHEN
SOLO.
IT'S SO HARD TO SAY GOODBYE, MY FRIEND.
I MANIFEST CIBLE IN YOUR LIFE, TO BE
GODSEND.
BUT FEAR NOT, FOR THE SUN WILL RISE,
MY LIFE IN POETRY, FOR YOU TO VISUALIZE.
GREET ME WITH A BRAND NEW DAWN.
DON'T STAY STAGNATE OR RETRO, LIFE GOES
ON.
IN THIS OUTRO, I HOPE YOU FOUND
CONSOLATION,
I PRAY THAT MY POEMS, INSPIRE EVERY
NATION.
THIS IS FIRST INSTALLMENT CURTAINS BEING
DRAWN.
FOR ENDINGS ARE NEW BEGINNINGS PAWN.

ABOUT THE AUTHOR

My name is Cue aka Grade A Cue. I was born in Jacksonville, Florida. My family was from the town Hilliard, Florida. I was youngest of 2 from my mother. I never met my biological father kids in person. I learned about them on Ancestry.com. All my life I Thought Eddie Lee Larry was my biological father. I still embrace him as Dad. And my Dad John Brown is who I raised by. I was into sports in my younger days, plus music. I eventually started gravitating towards music more, as my dreams of playing professional sports faded.
I was always into art. I drew a lot in my youngers days. Getting my drawings taking. Wasting up all my school paper. My Dad John Brown was in the Army so I moved around as a child. Staying in Kansas, Kentucky, Germany, California. When he got out the Army. I stayed in Hilliard, then Jacksonville, then Daytona Beach. After I graduated. I moved back to Jacksonville. I owned a music store called Grade A Enterprize for 21 years. Music became all downloading and streaming, so that kill my business. Now my new venture is being an author. This is the first installment of this series. My next project is called P.O.E.M.S. Product Of Environmental Maintaining Sustainability. I would talk more about me, but I'm basically telling you my life experiences in my writings. I hope you enjoyed the read. The next installment will be following up real soon.